amiguru ANIMAL HATS growing up

20 Crocheted Animal Hat Patterns for Ages 6-Adult

Linda Wright

In memory of my dog, Maggie, for the love and joy she brought to my life

Also by Linda Wright

Amigurumi Animal Hats

Amigurumi Holiday Hats for 18-Inch Dolls

Amigurumi Animal Hats for 18-Inch Dolls

Amigurumi Toilet Paper Covers

Toilet Paper Origami

Toilet Paper Origami On a Roll

Toilet Paper Crafts

Credits

Cover: Corrigan Speicher and John Wright

Photography: Randy and Linda Wright

Assistants: Ann Speicher, Mary Diehl and Shari Klintberg

Edition 2.0

Lindaloo Enterprises

P.O. Box 90135

Santa Barbara, California 93190

United States

sales@lindaloo.com

ISBN: 978-1-937564-99-5

Library of Congress Control Number: 2016903620

Contents

Introduction

Welcome to my menagerie! My first book of crocheted animal hat patterns was sized for babies and young children—and simply called *Amigurumi Animal Hats*. In this collection, the critters have grown up to fit ages 6 through adult. Some of my old animal friends are back—and this provides a way to make coordinating family outfits by using both books. Other animals are new...and I'm excited for you to meet them all!

Amigurumi (ah•mee•goo•roo•mee) is a Japanese term for cute crocheted animals. It is a colorful and cartoony style of stitchery that is tons of fun! Amigurumi is done by crocheting in a continuous spiral using one primary stitch—the single crochet—which makes it easy to master. I love the look of single crochet and it is also a tight stitch that works up into a thick fabric for a cozy hat.

These are mix-and-match patterns. Most of the hats have ear flaps while others have scarves that hang down over the ears. My patterns have been designed so that these elements can easily be interchanged. If you'd rather have ear flaps instead of scarves, or vice versa, it's easy to swap. Just follow the instructions in a pattern that has the feature you want. Furthermore, you can switch ear flap embellishments to your liking between twisted cords, pom poms and tassels...or even leave the ear flap's unadorned as I've done on the Bald Eagle, Turtle and Bee. Finally, ear flaps or scarves can be omitted altogether to make any hat as a beanie.

Thank you so much for buying *Amigurumi Animal Hats Growing Up!* I had such fun designing these patterns. May they bring much warmth and joy to you and yours!

General Directions

If you're new to crocheting, or if you need to brush up, the following pages include instructional diagrams for the stitches used in this book. If you like to learn by watching, YouTube.com is a treasure trove of excellent crocheting tutorials. To find what you need, just search on the stitch you want to learn. For example, magic ring crochet (also known as the magic circle or magic loop), single crochet, half double crochet, double crochet or loop stitch crochet.

For a hand-picked source of tutorials, I have assembled a collection of my favorites on Pinterest. You can view them at www.pinterest.com/LindalooEnt/ on a board named "Amigurumi Tutorials". There you can watch demonstrations for all of the stitches and techniques needed to make amigurumi animal hats.

In these patterns, you will be working with two strands of yarn held together. The multiple strands have the effect of a bulky yarn which makes a nice, warm hat and enables the hat to work up quickly. If you've never crocheted with multiple strands, just pretend you are working with a single strand and make each stitch as if you were holding one strand of yarn. That's really all there is to it. Buy 2 skeins of your main hat color (or 4 skeins for hats that include a scarf) and you'll be good to go! Some of the auxiliary pieces are made with a single strand.

Amigurumi is meant to be crocheted rather tightly. This will prevent fiberfill from showing through your stitches on any stuffed pieces. Be sure to check your gauge at the beginning of each pattern.

This book uses U.S. crochet terms. If an instruction says sc, that is a U.S. single crochet—or a U.K. double crochet. Please refer to the stitch diagrams on the following pages to be sure you are making the stitches as intended.

Hat Sizing

This book contains hat patterns in three sizes: Small (6 years-tween), Medium (teen-adult), and Large (large adult). Head sizes vary widely within age groups, so the best way to determine hat size is by measuring the head circumference and then selecting the size that most closely matches.

To measure a head's circumference, place a tape measure across the forehead, just above the ears, and measure over the hair around the full circumference of the head. Hold the measuring tape firmly, but not too tightly.

Size	Age	Head Circumference	Hat Circumference*
Small	6 yrs - Tween	18-20"	19"
Medium	Teen - Adult	20-22"	21"
Large	Large Adult	22-24"	23"

*Hat Circumference measurement is taken around inside edge of Hat.

Hats will stretch to fit a range of sizes. This allows for a snug fit. Some people like a looser fit, so take personal preference into consideration when choosing a size. Both of my cover models are wearing size Medium hats.

Supplies

Yarn

These hats were made with standard on-the-shelf yarns. Choose a soft worsted-weight yarn marked as number 4. Look on the label for the yarn weight symbol containing a "4" in the middle of a ball of yarn. I primarily used Lion Brand "Heartland" yarns. You will find my suggestions listed in the Resources section at the back of the book. Other yarns that I like are Red Heart "Soft", Lion Brand "Vanna's Choice" and Caron "Simply Soft". A yarn that is made of acrylic fibers, or acrylic blended with cotton or wool, is an ideal choice because the hat will be colorfast, washable and hold its shape well.

Scissors

You will need a small pair of sharp scissors.

Crochet Hook

The J10/6mm hook is used to make the hat base for all sizes and, depending on the hat size you are making, the following hooks are used for the extra features: F5/3.75mm, G6/4mm, H8/5mm, I9/5.5mm and K10.5/6.5mm. You may need to go up or down a hook size to obtain the gauge. My favorite hook is the Clover Soft Touch (below, center). I love the grip and the shape of the head which inserts easily into a stitch. Clover Soft Touch does not currently make a K10.5 and I like the Tulip Etimo for that size.

Yarn Needle

Yarn needles, or jumbo tapestry needles, have a large eye and a blunt point. They are made from metal or plastic. You will use one to sew the various pieces of your hat together and also to finish it off by weaving the loose ends into your work.

Stitch Markers

Stitch markers are used to keep track of where a round or row of crochet begins and ends. You can use a safety pin, bobby pin, paper clip or purchased stitch markers. I like the locking stitch markers that are shaped like safety pins. They are very secure and easy to use. Making the correct number of stitches is important, so count to double check if ever you're not sure.

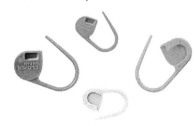

Animal Eyes

Plastic animal eyes work magic in bringing personality to these hats. They can be purchased at craft stores or online. A list of internet sources is included in the Resources section at the back of the book. One of my favorite sources, CR's Crafts, sells single sets in custom colors which makes it very economical to get just what you need. Each eye consists of a post section and a washer. To attach, work post into a gap between stitches. Place washer against post, lay eye against a hard surface and press washer firmly. In most patterns, the animal eye is attached to a crocheted rim, excess post is cut off and it is sewn to the hat. In several cases, where there is no crocheted rim, the entire post is cut off and the animal eye is hot glued to the hat. Buttons can be used as alternatives, if desired.

Wire Cutters

To clip excess post off of animal eyes.

Hot Glue Gun

A high temperature hot glue gun is used in several patterns to attach the eyes. I like to line hats with a piece of non-stick aluminum foil first in case a bit of glue drips through a gap between stitches. It's a good idea to practice with a spare eye on a scrap of crocheted fabric before gluing an eye to your hat. Hot glue makes a very permanent bond!

Disappearing Ink Marking Pen

This terrific marking tool can be helpful for marking the placement of eyes, ears, etc. Purchase it at a fabric store, craft store or online.

Straight Pins

Use standard dressmaker's pins or long corsage pins to hold pieces in place before sewing.

Ruler

For measuring and marking.

Sewing Needle & Thread

You will need these sewing box basics.

Hat Form

A hat form is helpful when it's time to pin a hat's finishing features in place. Large goblets and vases can be used. I've even set a cantaloupe, covered in plastic, on a wide-mouthed vase. Styrofoam mannequin heads are very economical and a 6" styrofoam ball works well.

Row Counter

Well worth the investment, a row counter keeps track of what round of the pattern you are crocheting. A pencil and paper can also be used.

Removable Notes

Use small sticky notes to keep track of your place in a pattern. Every time you complete a round or a row, move the note down to reveal the next line of instructions. I wouldn't work without one!

Stuffing

There are a few stuffed pieces in these patterns. Polyester fiberfill is my favorite stuffing material. This can be purchased by the bag at craft stores. One bag will go a long way! Scraps of yarn can also be used for stuffing small pieces.

Crochet Stitches

SLIP KNOT

This is used to make a starting loop on the crochet hook.

1. Make a loop about 5 inches from end of yarn. Insert hook in loop and hook onto supply yarn (yarn coming from ball) at A.

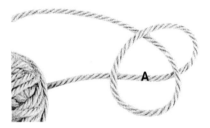

2. Pull yarn through loop.

3. Pull yarn ends to tighten loop around hook.

CHAIN (CH)

Start with a slip knot on hook.

1. Bring yarn **over** hook from back to front. Catch yarn with hook and pull it through the loop —

to look like this. One ch is done.

SINGLE CROCHET (SC)

This simple stitch is the primary stitch for amigurumi.

1. Insert hook in designated stitch. Note: Put hook under **both loops** that form v-shape at top of stitch unless otherwise instructed.

2. Yarn over and pull through the stitch (A).

You now have 2 loops on the hook:

3. Yarn over and pull through both loops on hook.

4. You now have 1 loop on hook and the sc stitch is done.

LOOP STITCH (LP ST)

The Loop Stitch is a variation of single crochet. The loops will form on the wrong side of the fabric (the side opposite the side you are facing). When the Loop Stitch is used for a hat, you will turn it wrong-side out when done. That way the loops will be on the outside — where you want them.

1. Insert hook in designated stitch, just as you do for a single crochet.

2. Wrap yarn around index finger of your yarn-holding hand to make a loop and lay loop on top of hook. Pull strands A and B through stitch C.

3. Yarn over and pull through all 3 loops on hook — A, B, and C.

4. The lp st is done.

HALF DOUBLE CROCHET (HDC)

1. Yarn over and insert hook in designated stitch.

2. Yarn over and pull through the stitch (A).

You now have 3 loops on hook:

3. Yarn over and pull through all 3 loops on hook (A, B & C).

4. You now have 1 loop on hook and the hdc stitch is done.

DOUBLE CROCHET (DC)

1. Yarn over and insert hook in designated stitch.

2. Yarn over and pull through the stitch (A).

You now have 3 loops on hook:

3. Yarn over and pull through 1st 2 loops on hook (A and B).

You now have 2 loops on hook:

4. Yarn over and pull through both loops on hook.

5. You now have 1 loop on hook and the dc stitch is done.

SINGLE CROCHET DECREASE (SC2TOG)

The instruction "sc2tog" means to use single crochet to join 2 stitches together. It is a way to decrease or make the item smaller.

1. Insert hook in stitch, yarn over and pull up a loop — to look like this:

2. Insert hook in next stitch, yarn over and pull up a loop — to look like this:

3. Yarn over and pull through all 3 loops on hook — to look like this. The sc2tog is done.

SLIP STITCH (SL ST)

1. Insert hook in stitch. Yarn over and pull through stitch and through loop on hook (A and B).

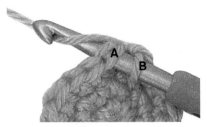

2. The sl st is done.

Techniques

★ MAGIC RING

Most all of my amigurumi begins with the magic ring. This is an adjustable loop that makes a neat center when crocheting in the round. If you're not familiar with it, you may want to watch a YouTube tutorial. It's not difficult — and well worth it. (An alternative to the magic ring, if desired, is to chain 2. Then begin Round 1 by working into the 2nd chain from the hook instead of the ring.)

1. Make a ring a few inches from end of yarn. Grasp ring between thumb and index finger where the join makes an X. Insert hook in ring, hook onto supply yarn at Y and pull up a loop —

to look like this.

2. Chain 1 —

to look like this. This chain does not count as a stitch.

3. Insert hook into ring so you're crocheting over ring and yarn tail. Pull up a loop to begin your first single crochet —

and complete the single crochet.

4. Continue to crochet over ring and yarn tail for the specified number of single crochets for the 1st round.

5. Pull tail to close up ring. To begin the 2nd round, insert hook in 1st stitch of 1st round (see arrow).

BEGIN 2ND RND HERE

WORKING IN THE ROUND

Working in the round means crocheting in a continuous spiral. Most amigurumi is worked in this manner.

USING STITCH MARKERS

It can be tricky to keep track of your place when working in the round, so be sure to use a stitch marker. The pattern will remind you! Place the stitch marker in the first stitch of a round — after completing the stitch. When you've crocheted all the way around, remove the stitch marker, make the next stitch, and replace the marker in the stitch just made. This will be the first stitch of the next round.

WORKING IN LOOPS

When a single crochet stitch is made, you will see 2 loops in a v-shape at the top of the stitch. To crochet the patterns in this book, insert your hook under **both loops** unless instructed otherwise. Crocheting in the "front loops only" or the "back loops only" is sometimes used for a different effect.

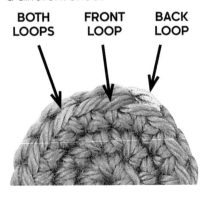

BOTH LOOPS   FRONT LOOP   BACK LOOP

MARKING THE EAR FLAPS OR SCARVES

The long tail is the center back of a Hat. To mark Ear Flaps or Scarves, count clockwise from long tail around rim of Hat and place 4 stitch markers as follows:

• For size **Small**, place markers in sts #7, 18, 43 and 54.

SIZE SMALL

Ear Flaps or Scarves are worked in green stitches.

• For size **Medium**, place markers in sts #7, 20, 47 and 60.

• For size **Large**, place markers in sts #7, 22, 51 and 66.

CHANGING COLORS

To change color while single crocheting, work last stitch of old color to last yarn over, yarn over with new color and pull through both loops to complete the stitch.

FASTENING OFF

This is the way to finish a piece so that it won't unravel. When you're done crocheting, cut the yarn and leave a tail. Wrap the tail over your hook and pull it all the way through the last loop left on your hook. Pull the tail tight and it will make a knot.

SMOOTHING THE EDGE

When fastening off, the knot can make a small bump in the edge of your work so that, for example, a round shape will not look as round as it should. To make the edge smooth, thread the long tail in a yarn needle and insert the needle down through the center "V" of the next stitch. This little step makes a big difference!

CLEANING

If you have used washable yarn, your hat will be easy to clean. Follow the laundry care instructions on the yarn label and wash as directed. Lay flat to dry.

TWISTED CORD TIE

The 16 yarn strands are pulled through Ear Flaps in groups of 4.

1. With crochet hook, catch 4 yarn strands at the center and pull through tip of Ear Flap —

then pull 1 side of loop all the way through to look like this:

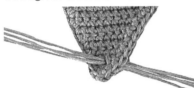

2. Pull next 4 strands through in same manner.

3. Repeat 2 more times, like this...

and this...

...until all strands are pulled thru tip of Ear Flap as shown below:

Be sure all ends are even when hanging straight down.

4. Place hat on a firm surface and weigh it down with a heavy book. Divide yarn into 2 groups of 16 strands. If 2 colors are used, make each group the same color.

5. Hold a group in each hand grasping about 2 inches from Ear Flap — and twist yarn to the **right**.

6. When yarn has a good tight twist, wrap **right group over left group —**

and wrap **right over left** a few more times until all twisted yarn is wrapped.

7. Move your hands down 2 more inches, twist yarn and repeat Step 6. Continue twisting and wrapping until near end of strands. Tie all strands together with an overhand knot 15 inches from tip of Ear Flap. Trim ends even.

FRINGE TECHNIQUE

1. Follow pattern instructions for length and quantity of yarn strands to be used. Put hook through desired stitch, catch strand(s) in the middle and pull part way through stitch to make a loop. (Photos below show fringe being made with 2 yarn strands.)

2. With hook in loop, lay yarn ends over hook.

3. Pull yarn ends all the way through loop. Take hold of ends and pull tight.

COUNTING ROUNDS

Periodically, it is good to count your rounds to ensure your place in a pattern. Fortunately, rounds are clearly defined and counting is easy. Each round makes a ridge. A groove separates the rounds. You need only to count the ridges. Take a look at the photo below to see that the circle has 5 rounds.

ASSEMBLING

The assembly stage of amigurumi hat making is an exciting time. This is when all pieces are sewn together and the project blossoms in cuteness! Thread a yarn needle with the long tail of your auxiliary piece (ear, eye rim, beak, etc.) and use a whip stitch or running stitch to sew it to the hat. It's good to temporarily pin your pieces in place beforehand to decide where you like them the best. A sewing needle and thread can also be used to sew feature pieces onto your hat and in some cases it will make the stitches less visible.

WEAVING IN ENDS

The final assembly instruction for every pattern is to weave in the ends. This is the way to hide and secure all of your straggly yarn tails. Thread the yarn end into a yarn needle, then skim through the back of the stitches on the wrong side of your work. Continue for about 2 inches, then turn and double back to lock the yarn into place. Trim the end close. When you turn your work to the right side, you should not see the woven ends. They should be tucked into the middle of your crocheted fabric.

ATTACHING WITH SC

Put yarn on hook with Slip Knot. Insert hook in indicated stitch. Complete sc as shown in Single Crochet tutorial, page 10 steps 2-4.

Embroidery Stitches

STRAIGHT STITCH

A simple, single stitch. Come up from wrong side of fabric at A and go down at B.

A   B

RUNNING STITCH

The Running Stitch is formed by a detached series of Straight Stitches. Make it by running the needle up and down the fabric at a regular distance. Come up at A, down at B, up at C, down at D, up at E, down at F, etc.

A   B   C   D   E   F

CHAIN STITCH EMBROIDERY

1. Bring needle up from wrong side at A. Put needle back in at A and out at B, but don't pull the needle completely through.

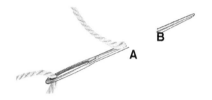

2. Wrap yarn around needle from left to right to form a loop.

3. Pull needle out to tighten loop. First stitch is done.

4. Put needle in at B and out at C. Repeat Steps 2 and 3 to complete 2nd stitch. Continue to make as many stitches as needed.

How to Measure your Gauge

Gauge is written as follows.

With J10/6mm hook and 2 strands of yarn held together:
5 rnds of sc = 3" diameter circle

This means that when you've crocheted the first 5 rounds of single crochet on a piece, the circle (or hexagon) you've created should have a 3" diameter. So, when you have crocheted the first 5 founds of a hat, measure it. If your measurement is 3", your hat will conform with the Hat Sizing Chart on page 7. To alter your gauge, adjust your crochet tension (tightness) or change to a larger or smaller crochet hook. It is very common for gauge to vary from person to person.

Abbreviations

Crochet patterns are written using abbreviations that save space and make the patterns easier to read. The following abbreviations are used:

st	stitch		**sl st**	slip stitch
ch	chain		**rnd**	round
sc	single crochet		**sc2tog**	single crochet decrease
hdc	half double crochet		**yd**	yard
dc	double crochet		* *	a set of sts
lp st	loop stitch		( )	stitch count

How to Read a Pattern

The directions are for written for size Small. Changes for sizes Medium and Large are in brackets separated by a semi-colon, for example, [Medium; Large]. Each round or row is written on a new line. Most rounds have a repeated set of instructions that are written between two asterisks *like this*. The set is to be repeated as many times as indicated before you move on to the next step. A set can also be done all in one stitch if indicated after the asterisks. At the end of a round, the total number of stitches to be made in that round is indicated in parentheses (like this).

Let's look at a round from a hat:

Rnd 6: *sc in next 4 sts, 2 sc in next st* 6 times (36 sts).

This means:

Rnd 6	This is the 6th round of the pattern.
sc in next 4 sts	Make 1 single crochet stitch in each of the next 4 stitches
2 sc in next st	Make 2 single crochet stitches, both in the same stitch
6 times	Repeat everything between * and * 6 times.
(36 sts)	The round will have a total of 36 stitches.

So, following the instructions for Round 6, you will:

single crochet in the next 4 sts, 2 sc in the next st,
single crochet in the next 4 sts, 2 sc in the next st,
single crochet in the next 4 sts, 2 sc in the next st,
single crochet in the next 4 sts, 2 sc in the next st,
single crochet in the next 4 sts, 2 sc in the next st,
single crochet in the next 4 sts, 2 sc in the next st,

for a total of 36 stitches.

rhinoceros

SIZES

Small [Medium; Large]

SUPPLIES

Worsted weight yarn in gray 485 yds [620; 690] and light gray 60 yds

G6/4mm, H8/5mm and J10/6mm [H8/5mm and J10/6mm; I9/5.5mm, J10/6mm and K10.5/6.5mm] crochet hooks or size needed to obtain gauge

2 black animal eyes, 15mm

Wire cutters

Stuffing

Stitch marker

Yarn needle

GAUGE

With J10/6mm hook and 2 strands of yarn held together:

5 rnds of sc = 3" diameter circle

HAT

With J10/6mm hook and 2 strands of gray yarn held together, make a magic ring, ch 1.

Rnd 1: 6 sc in ring, pull ring closed tight (6 sts).

Rnd 2: 2 sc in each st around. Place marker for beginning of rnd and move marker up as each rnd is completed (12 sts).

Rnd 3: *sc in next st, 2 sc in next st* 6 times (18 sts).

Rnd 4: *sc in next 2 sts, 2 sc in next st* 6 times (24 sts).

Rnd 5: *sc in next 3 sts, 2 sc in next st* 6 times (30 sts).

Rnd 6: *sc in next 4 sts, 2 sc in next st* 6 times (36 sts).

Rnd 7: *sc in next 5 sts, 2 sc in next st* 6 times (42 sts).

Rnd 8: *sc in next 6 sts, 2 sc in next st* 6 times (48 sts).

Rnd 9: *sc in next 7 sts, 2 sc in next st* 6 times (54 sts).

Rnd 10: *sc in next 8 sts, 2 sc in next st* 6 times (60 sts).

• FOR SIZE SMALL:

Rnds 11-25: sc in each st around. Fasten off.

• FOR SIZE MEDIUM:

Rnd 11: *sc in next 9 sts, 2 sc in next st* 6 times (66 sts).

Rnds 12-27: sc in each st around. Fasten off.

• FOR SIZE LARGE:

Rnd 11: *sc in next 9 sts, 2 sc in next st* 6 times (66 sts).

Rnd 12: *sc in next 10 sts, 2 sc in next st* 6 times (72 sts).

Rnds 13-29: sc in each st around. Fasten off.

SCARF (MAKE 2)

Mark position of Scarf (see page 14). Work Scarf into sts between markers, not including marked sts.

• **For size Small,** work in the 10 sts between each set of markers.

• **For size Medium,** work in the 12 sts between each set of markers.

• **For size Large,** work in the 14 sts between each set of markers.

Note: A chain 1 at the beginning of a row is for turning your work and does not count as a stitch.

Row 1: With J10/6mm hook and 2 strands of gray yarn held together, attach yarn in 1st st with sc, sc in each remaining st across. Place marker for beginning of row and move marker up as each row is completed.

Row 2: ch 1, turn, sc in each st across.

Rows 3-end: Repeat Row 2 until scarf is about 20" long.

EDGE TRIM

Using J10/6mm hook and 2 strands of gray yarn held together, attach yarn at center back of Hat with sc. Sc in each st around perimeter of Hat and Scarves making 3 sts in same st at lower corners of Scarves. Fasten off.

TOES

Use J10/6mm hook and 2 strands of light gray yarn held together.

• FOR SIZE SMALL:

Work into the 12 sts on Scarf ends.

Toe 1: fasten on, ch 2 and dc in 1st st; dc in next st; dc, ch 2 and sl st in next st; sl st in next st.

Toe 2: sl st, ch 2 and dc in next st; dc in next 2 sts; dc, ch 2 and sl st in next st; sl st in next st.

Toe 3: sl st, ch 2 and dc in next st; dc in next st; dc, ch 2 and sl st in next st. Fasten off.

• FOR SIZE MEDIUM:

Work into the 14 sts on Scarf ends.

Toe 1: fasten on, ch 2 and dc in 1st st; dc in next st; dc, ch 2 and sl st in next st; sl st in next st.

Toe 2: sl st, ch 2 and dc in next st; dc in next 4 sts; dc, ch 2 and sl st in next st; sl st in next st.

Toe 3: sl st, ch 2 and dc in next st; dc in next st; dc, ch 2 and sl st in next st. Fasten off.

• FOR SIZE LARGE:

Work into the 16 sts on Scarf ends.

Toe 1: fasten on, ch 2 and dc in 1st st; dc in next 2 sts; dc, ch 2 and sl st in next st; sl st in next st.

Toe 2: sl st, ch 2 and dc in next st; dc in next 4 sts; dc, ch 2 and sl st in next st; sl st in next st.

Toe 3: sl st, ch 2 and dc in next st; dc in next st 2 sts; dc, ch 2 and sl st in next st. Fasten off.

EYE RIM (MAKE 2)

Work in back loops only. With G6/4mm [H8/5mm; I9/5.5mm] hook and a single strand of gray yarn, make a magic ring, ch 1.

Rnd 1: 6 sc in ring, pull ring closed almost tight (6 sts).

Rnd 2: 2 sc in each st around. Place marker for beginning of rnd and move marker up as each rnd is completed (12 sts).

Rnd 3: *sc in next st, 2 sc in next st* 6 times (18 sts).

Rnd 4: *sc in next 2 sts, 2 sc in next st* 6 times (24 sts).

Rnd 5: *sc in next 3 sts, 2 sc in next st* 6 times (30 sts).

Fasten off with long tail.

EAR (MAKE 2)

With hook size H8/5mm [J10/6mm; K10.5/6.5mm] and 2 strands of gray yarn held together, make a magic ring, ch 1.

Rnd 1: 6 sc in ring, pull ring closed tight (6 sts).

Rnd 2: 2 sc in each st around. Place marker for beginning of rnd and move marker up as each rnd is completed (12 sts).

Rnd 3: sc in each st around.

Rnd 4: *sc in next st, 2 sc in next st* 6 times (18 sts).

Rnd 5: *sc in next 2 sts, 2 sc in next st* 6 times (24 sts).

Rnd 6: *sc in next 3 sts, 2 sc in next st* 6 times (30 sts).

Rnd 7: *sc in next 4 sts, 2 sc in next st* 6 times (36 sts).

Rnds 8-12: sc in each st around.

Fasten off with long tail.

Flatten Ear as shown in Fig. A.

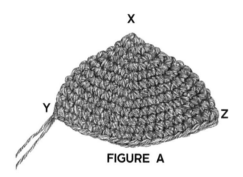

FIGURE A

Pinch at X to make a nice point. Use 1 strand of tail to sew layers together from Y to Z. Tie tails together so that Y meets Z and knot securely.

LARGE HORN

With G6/4mm [H8/5mm; I9/5.5mm] hook and a single strand of light gray yarn, make a magic ring, ch 1.

Rnd 1: 5 sc in ring, pull ring closed tight (5 sts).

Rnd 2: sc in next 4 sts, 2 sc in next st (6 sts).

Rnd 3: sc in next 5 sts, 2 sc in next st (7 sts).

Rnd 4: sc in next 6 sts, 2 sc in next st (8 sts).

Rnd 5: *sc in next 3 sts, 2 sc in next st* 2 times (10 sts).

Rnd 6: *sc in next 4 sts, 2 sc in next st* 2 times (12 sts).

Rnd 7: sc in each st around.

Rnd 8: *sc in next 5 sts, 2 sc in next st* 2 times (14 sts).

Rnd 9: sc in each st around.

Rnd 10: *sc in next 6 sts, 2 sc in next st* 2 times (16 sts).

Rnd 11: sc in each st around.

Rnd 12: *sc in next 7 sts, 2 sc in next st* 2 times (18 sts).

Rnd 13: sc in each st around.

Rnd 14: *sc in next 8 sts, 2 sc in next st* 2 times (20 sts).

Rnd 15: sc in each st around.

Rnd 16: *sc in next 9 sts, 2 sc in next st* 2 times (22 sts).

Rnd 17: sc in each st around.

Rnd 18: *sc in next 10 sts, 2 sc in next st* 2 times (24 sts).

Rnd 19: sc in each st around.

Rnd 20: *sc in next 11 sts, 2 sc in next st* 2 times (26 sts).

Rnd 21-22: sc in each st around.

Rnd 23: *sc in next 12 sts, 2 sc in next st* 2 times (28 sts).

Rnd 24-28: sc in each st around.

Fasten off with long tail.

Stuff with fiberfill. With yarn needle, run long tail through stitches from base of long tail to tip of Horn, passing through the actual stitches, not through the stuffing (see Fig. B). Pull long tail like a drawstring to shape Horn into a curve, knot to hold shape, and run needle back through Horn to opening edge.

Note: A small v-shaped notch in edge of Horn may appear at base of drawstring. If so, close it up with a stitch or two.

FIGURE B

SMALL HORN

With G6/4mm [H8/5mm; I9/5.5mm] hook and a single strand of light gray yarn, make a magic ring, ch 1.

Rnd 1: 5 sc in ring, pull ring closed tight (5 sts).

Rnd 2: sc in next 4 sts, 2 sc in next st (6 sts).

Rnd 3: sc in next 5 sts, 2 sc in next st (7 sts).

Rnd 4: sc in next 6 sts, 2 sc in next st (8 sts).

Rnd 5: *sc in next 3 sts, 2 sc in next st* 2 times (10 sts).

Rnd 6: *sc in next 4 sts, 2 sc in next st* 2 times (12 sts).

Rnd 7: sc in each st around.

Rnd 8: *sc in next 5 sts, 2 sc in next st* 2 times (14 sts).

Rnd 9: sc in each st around.

Rnd 10: *sc in next 6 sts, 2 sc in next st* 2 times (16 sts).

Rnd 11: sc in each st around.

Rnd 12: *sc in next 7 sts, 2 sc in next st* 2 times (18 sts).

Rnd 13: sc in each st around.

Fasten off with long tail.

Stuff and shape into a curve following instructions for Large Horn.

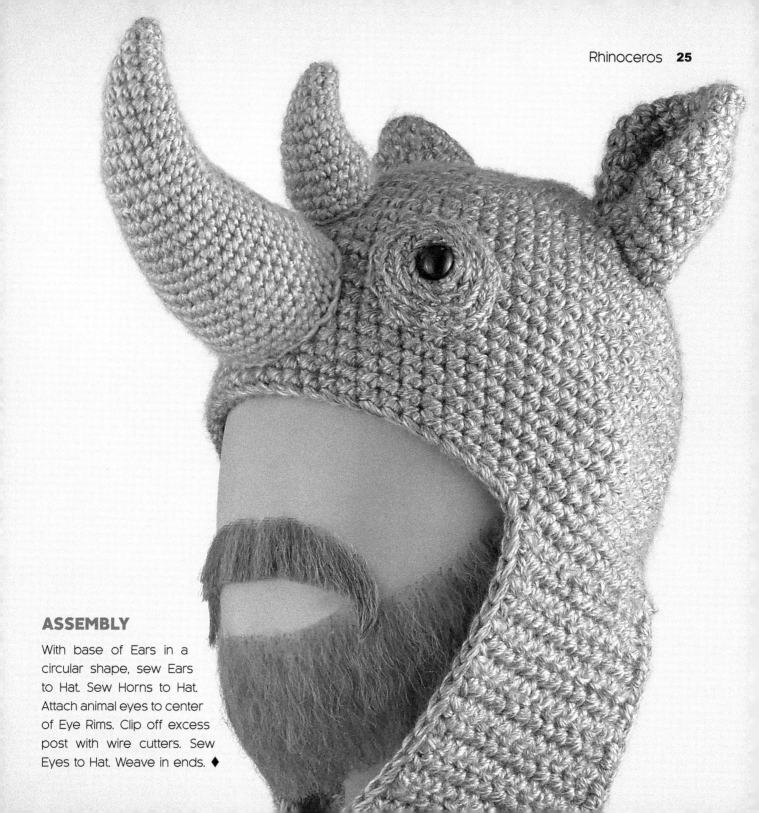

ASSEMBLY

With base of Ears in a circular shape, sew Ears to Hat. Sew Horns to Hat. Attach animal eyes to center of Eye Rims. Clip off excess post with wire cutters. Sew Eyes to Hat. Weave in ends. ♦

flamingo

SIZES

Small [Medium; Large]

SUPPLIES

Worsted weight yarn in pink 210 yds [270; 300]; hot pink 50 yds; plus small amount of white and black

G6/4mm, H8/5mm and J10/6mm [H8/5mm and J10/6mm; H8/5mm, I9/5.5mm and J10/6mm] crochet hooks or size needed to obtain gauge

2 yellow animal eyes, 24mm

Wire cutters

Stuffing

Stitch marker

Yarn needle

GAUGE

With J10/6mm hook and 2 strands of yarn held together:

5 rnds of sc = 3" diameter circle

HAT

With J10/6mm hook and 2 strands of pink yarn held together, make a magic ring, ch 1.

Rnd 1: 6 sc in ring, pull ring closed tight (6 sts).

Rnd 2: 2 sc in each st around. Place marker for beginning of rnd and move marker up as each rnd is completed (12 sts).

Rnd 3: *sc in next st, 2 sc in next st* 6 times (18 sts).

Rnd 4: *sc in next 2 sts, 2 sc in next st* 6 times (24 sts).

Rnd 5: *sc in next 3 sts, 2 sc in next st* 6 times (30 sts).

Rnd 6: *sc in next 4 sts, 2 sc in next st* 6 times (36 sts).

Rnd 7: *sc in next 5 sts, 2 sc in next st* 6 times (42 sts).

Rnd 8: *sc in next 6 sts, 2 sc in next st* 6 times (48 sts).

Rnd 9: *sc in next 7 sts, 2 sc in next st* 6 times (54 sts).

Rnd 10: *sc in next 8 sts, 2 sc in next st* 6 times (60 sts).

• FOR SIZE SMALL:

Rnds 11-25: sc in each st around. Fasten off.

• FOR SIZE MEDIUM:

Rnd 11: *sc in next 9 sts, 2 sc in next st* 6 times (66 sts).

Rnds 12-27: sc in each st around. Fasten off.

• FOR SIZE LARGE:

Rnd 11: *sc in next 9 sts, 2 sc in next st* 6 times (66 sts).

Rnd 12: *sc in next 10 sts, 2 sc in next st* 6 times (72 sts).

Rnds 13-29: sc in each st around. Fasten off.

EAR FLAP (MAKE 2)

Mark position of Ear Flaps (see page 14). Work Ear Flaps into sts between markers, not including the marked sts.

• **For size Small,** work in the 10 sts between each set of markers.

• **For size Medium,** work in the 12 sts between each set of markers.

• **For size Large,** work in the 14 sts between each set of markers.

Note: A chain 1 at the beginning of a row is for turning your work and does not count as a stitch.

Row 1: With J10/6mm hook and 2 strands of pink yarn held together, attach yarn in 1st st with sc, sc in each remaining st across. Place marker for beginning of row and move marker up as each row is completed.

Row 2: ch 1, turn, skip next st, sc in each remaining st across.

Rows 3-end: Repeat Row 2 until only 3 sc remain, ch 1, turn, insert hook in each st and pull up a loop. You will have 4 loops on hook. Yarn over and pull through all 4 loops. Fasten off. Weave in ends.

EDGE TRIM

With J10/6mm hook and 2 strands of pink yarn held together, attach yarn at center back of Hat with sc. Sc in each st around perimeter of Hat making 3 sts in same st at tip of each Ear Flap. Fasten off.

TWISTED CORD TIE (MAKE 2)

Cut sixteen 54" strands of hot pink yarn. Follow instructions on page 15.

BEAK

With G6/4mm [H8/5mm; I9/5.5mm] hook and a single strand of black yarn, make a magic ring, ch 1.

Rnd 1: 5 sc in ring, pull ring closed tight (5 sts).

Rnd 2: sc in next 4 sts, 2 sc in next st (6 sts).

Rnd 3: sc in next 5 sts, 2 sc in next st (7 sts).

Rnd 4: sc in next 6 sts, 2 sc in next st (8 sts).

Rnd 5: *sc in next 3 sts, 2 sc in next st* 2 times (10 sts).

Rnd 6: *sc in next 4 sts, 2 sc in next st* 2 times (12 sts).

Rnd 7: sc in each st around.

Rnd 8: *sc in next 5 sts, 2 sc in next st* 2 times (14 sts).

Rnd 9: sc in each st around.

Rnd 10: *sc in next 6 sts, 2 sc in next st* 2 times (16 sts).

Rnd 11: sc in each st around.

Rnd 12: *sc in next 7 sts, 2 sc in next st* 2 times (18 sts).

Rnd 13: sc in each st around; change to white yarn in last st.

Rnd 14: *sc in next 8 sts, 2 sc in next st* 2 times (20 sts).

Rnd 15: sc in each st around.

Rnd 16: *sc in next 9 sts, 2 sc in next st* 2 times (22 sts).

Rnd 17: sc in each st around.

Rnd 18: *sc in next 10 sts, 2 sc in next st* 2 times (24 sts).

Rnd 19: sc in each st around.

Rnd 20: *sc in next 11 sts, 2 sc in next st* 2 times (26 sts).

Rnd 21-22: sc in each st around.

Rnd 23: *sc in next 12 sts, 2 sc in next st* 2 times (28 sts).

Rnd 24-28: sc in each st around.

Fasten off with long tail. Stuff with fiberfill. With yarn needle, run long tail through stitches from base of long tail to tip of Beak, passing through the actual stitches, not through the stuffing (refer to Fig. B photo, page 23). Pull long tail like a drawstring to shape Beak into a curve, knot to hold shape, and run needle back through Beak to opening edge.

Note: A small v-shaped notch in edge of Beak may appear at base of drawstring. If so, close it up with a stitch or two.

EYE RIM (MAKE 2)

With H8/5mm crochet hook and a single strand of white yarn, make a magic ring, ch 1.

Rnd 1: 6 sc in ring, pull ring almost tight (6 sts).

Rnd 2: 2 sc in each st around. Place marker for beginning of rnd and move marker up as each rnd is completed (12 sts).

Rnd 3: *2 sc in next st, sc in next st* 6 times (18 sts).

Sl st in next st. Fasten off with long tail.

ASSEMBLY

With black yarn, embroider 2 straight sts on Beak, about 1" long, for nostrils. Sew Beak to Hat. Attach animal eyes to center of Eye Rims. Clip off excess post with wire cutters. Sew Eyes to Hat. Weave in ends. ♦

turtle

SIZES

Small [Medium; Large]

SUPPLIES

Worsted weight yarn in dark green 195 yds [250; 275] and light green 100 yds [130; 145]

G6/4mm, H8/5mm and J10/6mm [H8/5mm and J10/6mm; H8/5mm, I9/5.5mm and J10/6mm] crochet hooks or size needed to obtain gauge

2 green animal/cat eyes, 12mm

Stuffing

Stitch marker

Yarn needle

GAUGE

With J10/6mm hook and 2 strands of yarn held together:

5 rnds of sc = 3" diameter circle

HAT

With J10/6mm hook and 2 strands of dark green yarn held together, make a magic ring, ch 1.

Rnd 1: 6 sc in ring, pull ring closed tight (6 sts).

Rnd 2: 2 sc in each st around. Place marker for beginning of rnd and move marker up as each rnd is completed (12 sts).

Rnd 3: *sc in next st, 2 sc in next st* 6 times (18 sts).

Rnd 4: *sc in next 2 sts, 2 sc in next st* 6 times (24 sts).

Rnd 5: *sc in next 3 sts, 2 sc in next st* 6 times (30 sts).

Rnd 6: *sc in next 4 sts, 2 sc in next st* 6 times (36 sts).

Rnd 7: *sc in next 5 sts, 2 sc in next st* 6 times (42 sts).

Rnd 8: *sc in next 6 sts, 2 sc in next st* 6 times (48 sts).

Rnd 9: *sc in next 7 sts, 2 sc in next st* 6 times (54 sts).

Rnd 10: *sc in next 8 sts, 2 sc in next st* 6 times (60 sts).

• FOR SIZE SMALL:

Rnds 11-19: sc in each st around; change to light green yarn in last st.

Rnd 20: working in back loops only, sc in each st around.

Rnds 21-25: resume working in both loops. Sc in each st around. Fasten off.

• FOR SIZE MEDIUM:

Rnd 11: *sc in next 9 sts, 2 sc in next st* 6 times (66 sts).

Rnds 12-21: sc in each st around; change to light green yarn in last st.

Rnd 22: working in back loops only, sc in each st around.

Rnds 23-27: resume working in both loops. Sc in each st around. Fasten off.

• FOR SIZE LARGE:

Rnd 11: *sc in next 9 sts, 2 sc in next st* 6 times (66 sts).

Rnd 12: *sc in next 10 sts, 2 sc in next st* 6 times (72 sts).

Rnds 13-23: sc in each st around; change to light green yarn in last st.

Rnd 24: working in back loops only, sc in each st around.

Rnds 25-29: resume working in both loops. Sc in each st around. Fasten off.

EAR FLAP (MAKE 2)

Mark position of Ear Flaps (see page 14). Work Ear Flaps into sts between markers, not including the marked sts.

• **For size Small,** work in the 10 sts between each set of markers.

• **For size Medium,** work in the 12 sts between each set of markers.

- **For size Large,** work in the 14 sts between each set of markers.

Note: A chain 1 at the beginning of a row is for turning your work and does not count as a stitch.

Row 1: With J10/6mm hook and 2 strands of light green yarn held together, attach yarn in 1st st with sc, sc in each remaining st across. Place marker for beginning of row and move marker up as each row is completed.

Row 2: ch 1, turn, skip next st, sc in each remaining st across.

Rows 3-end: Repeat Row 2 until only 3 sc remain, ch 1, turn, insert hook in each st and pull up a loop. You will have 4 loops on hook. Yarn over and pull through all 4 loops.

Fasten off. Weave in ends.

EDGE TRIM

Using J10/6mm hook and 2 strands of dark green yarn held together, attach yarn at center back of Hat with sc. Sc in each st around perimeter of Hat making 3 sts in same st at tip of each Ear Flap. Fasten off.

SHELL RIM

To crochet the Shell Rim, fold edge of Hat inward along line where dark green meets light green.

Use J10/6mm hook and 2 strands of dark green yarn held together.

• FOR SIZE SMALL:

Attach yarn with sc at center back of Hat in an unworked front loop of Rnd 20 (counts as 1st st of Rnd 1).

Rnd 1: *sc in next 9 sts, 2 sc in next st* 6 times. Place marker for beginning of rnd and move marker up as each rnd is completed (66 sts).

Rnd 2: *sc in next 10 sts, 2 sc in next st* 6 times (72 sts).

Rnd 3: *sc in next 11 sts, 2 sc in next st* 6 times (78 sts).

Rnd 4: *sc in next 12 sts, 2 sc in next st* 6 times (84 sts).

Sl st in next st. Fasten off.

• FOR SIZE MEDIUM:

Attach yarn with sc at center back of Hat in an unworked front loop of Rnd 22 (counts as 1st st of Rnd 1).

Rnd 1: *sc in next 10 sts, 2 sc in next st* 6 times. Place marker for beginning of rnd and move marker up as each rnd is completed (72 sts).

Rnd 2: *sc in next 11 sts, 2 sc in next st* 6 times (78 sts).

Rnd 3: *sc in next 12 sts, 2 sc in next st* 6 times (84 sts).

Rnd 4: *sc in next 13 sts, 2 sc in next st* 6 times (90 sts).

Sl st in next st. Fasten off.

• FOR SIZE LARGE:

Attach yarn with sc at center back of Hat in an unworked front loop of Rnd 24 (counts as 1st st of Rnd 1).

Rnd 1: *sc in next 11 sts, 2 sc in next st* 6 times. Place marker for beginning of rnd and move marker up as each rnd is completed (78 sts).

Rnd 2: *sc in next 12 sts, 2 sc in next st* 6 times 84 sts).

Rnd 3: *sc in next 13 sts, 2 sc in next st* 6 times (90 sts).

Rnd 4: *sc in next 14 sts, 2 sc in next st* 6 times (96 sts).

Sl st in next st. Fasten off.

PENTAGON

With G6/4mm [H8/5mm; I9/5.5mm] hook and a single strand of dark green yarn, make a magic ring, ch 1.

Rnd 1: 5 sc in ring, pull ring closed tight (5 sts).

Rnd 2: 2 sc in each st around. Place marker for beginning of rnd and move marker up as each rnd is completed (10 sts).

Rnd 3: *sc in next st, 3 sc in next st* 5 times (20 sts).

Rnd 4: sc in each st around change to light green yarn in last st.

Rnd 5: sc in next 2 sts, 3 sc in next st, *sc in next 3 sts, 3 sc in next st* 4 times, sc in next st (30 sts).

Rnd 6: sc in each st around.

Rnd 7: sc in next 3 sts, 3 sc in next st, *sc in next 5 sts, 3 sc in next st* 4 times, sc in next 2 sts (40 sts).

Sl st in next st. Fasten off with long tail.

HEXAGON (MAKE 5)

With G6/4mm [H8/5mm; I9/5.5mm] hook and a single strand of dark green yarn, make a magic ring, ch 1.

Rnd 1: 6 sc in ring, pull ring closed tight (6 sts).

Rnd 2: 2 sc in each st around. Place marker for beginning of rnd and move marker up as each rnd is completed (12 sts).

Rnd 3: *sc in next st, 3 sc in next st* 6 times (24 sts).

Rnd 4: sc in each st around; change to light green yarn in last st.

Rnd 5: sc in next 2 sts, 3 sc in next st, *sc in next 3 sts, 3 sc in next st* 5 times, sc in next st (36 sts).

Rnd 6: sc in each st around.

Rnd 7: sc in next 3 sts, 3 sc in next st, *sc in next 5 sts, 3 sc in next st* 5 times, sc in next 2 sts (48 sts).

Sl st in next st. Fasten off with long tail.

HEAD

With H8/5mm hook and a single strand of light green yarn, make a magic ring, ch 1.

Rnd 1: 6 sc in ring, pull ring closed tight (6 sts).

Rnd 2: 2 sc in each st around. Place marker for beginning of rnd and move marker up as each rnd is completed (12 sts).

Rnd 3: *sc in next st, 2 sc in next st* 6 times (18 sts).

Rnds 4-8: sc in each st around. Fasten off with long tail.

TAIL

With H8/5mm hook and a single strand of light green yarn, make a magic ring, ch 1.

Rnd 1: 4 sc in ring, pull ring closed tight (4 sts).

Rnd 2: sc in next 3 sts, 2 sc in next st (5 sts).

Rnd 3: sc in next 4 sts, 2 sc in next st (6 sts).

Rnd 4: sc in next 5 sts, 2 sc in next st (7 sts).

Rnd 5: sc in next 6 sts, 2 sc in next st (8 sts).

Rnd 6: sc in next 7 sts, 2 sc in next st (9 sts).

Rnd 7: sc in next 8 sts, 2 sc in next st (10 sts).

Rnd 8: sc in next 9 sts, 2 sc in next st (11 sts).

Rnd 9: sc in next 10 sts, 2 sc in next st (12 sts).

Fasten off with long tail.

ASSEMBLY

Sew Pentagon to top of Hat. Sew Hexagons around side of Hat. Attach animal eyes to Head. Stuff Head and sew to front of Hat. Flatten Tail and sew to back of Hat (under Shell Rim, where Shell Rim meets Hat). Weave in ends. ◆

octopus

SIZES

Small [Medium; Large]

SUPPLIES

Worsted weight yarn in aqua 375 yds [480; 535]; plus small amount of off-white

H8/5mm and J10/6mm [H8/5mm and J10/6mm; H8/5mm, J10/6mm and K10.5/6.5mm] crochet hooks or size needed to obtain gauge

2 black animal eyes, 24mm

Wire cutters

Stitch marker

Yarn needle

GAUGE

With J10/6mm hook and 2 strands of yarn held together:

5 rnds of sc = 3" diameter circle

HAT

With J10/6mm hook and 2 strands of aqua yarn held together, make a magic ring, ch 1.

Rnd 1: 6 sc in ring, pull ring closed tight (6 sts).

Rnd 2: 2 sc in each st around. Place marker for beginning of rnd and move marker up as each rnd is completed (12 sts).

Rnd 3: *sc in next st, 2 sc in next st* 6 times (18 sts).

Rnd 4: *sc in next 2 sts, 2 sc in next st* 6 times (24 sts).

Rnd 5: *sc in next 3 sts, 2 sc in next st* 6 times (30 sts).

Rnd 6: *sc in next 4 sts, 2 sc in next st* 6 times (36 sts).

Rnd 7: *sc in next 5 sts, 2 sc in next st* 6 times (42 sts).

Rnd 8: *sc in next 6 sts, 2 sc in next st* 6 times (48 sts).

Rnd 9: *sc in next 7 sts, 2 sc in next st* 6 times (54 sts).

Rnd 10: *sc in next 8 sts, 2 sc in next st* 6 times (60 sts).

• **FOR SIZE SMALL:**

Rnds 11-26: sc in each st around. Fasten off.

• **FOR SIZE MEDIUM:**

Rnd 11: *sc in next 9 sts, 2 sc in next st* 6 times (66 sts).

Rnds 12-28: sc in each st around. Fasten off.

• **FOR SIZE LARGE:**

Rnd 11: *sc in next 9 sts, 2 sc in next st* 6 times (66 sts).

Rnd 12: *sc in next 10 sts, 2 sc in next st* 6 times (72 sts).

Rnds 13-30: sc in each st around. Fasten off.

EYE RIM (MAKE 2)

With H8/5mm hook and a single strand of off-white yarn, make a magic ring, ch 1.

Rnd 1: 6 sc in ring, pull ring closed almost tight (6 sts).

Rnd 2: 2 sc in each st around. Place marker for beginning of rnd and move marker up as each rnd is completed (12 sts).

Rnd 3: *sc in next st, 2 sc in next st* 6 times (18 sts).

Fasten off with long tail.

ARM (MAKE 8)

With hook size H8/5mm [J10/6mm; K10.5/6.5mm] and 2 strands of aqua yarn held together, ch 63 loosely.

Note: A chain 1 at the beginning of a row is for turning your work and does not count as a stitch.

Row 1: starting in 2nd ch from hook, sl st in next 2 ch, sc in next 20 ch, hdc in next 20 ch, dc in next 20 ch. Place marker for beginning of row and move marker up as each row is completed (62 sts).

Row 2: ch 1, turn, sc in each st across (62 sts).

Row 3: ch 1, turn, sl st in next 2 sts, sc in next 20 sts, hdc in next 20 sts, dc in next 20 sts (62 sts).

One arm is done. Without cutting the yarn, ch 63 loosely and repeat Rows 1-3 to make 7 more Arms. Fasten off with long tail.

You will end up with 8 Arms connected in a row.

ASSEMBLY

Pin row of Legs to back half of Hat, right sides together, matching center of leg strip to center back of Hat and adjusting to fit. Sew in place. Attach animal eyes to center of Eye Rims. Clip off excess post with wire cutters. Sew eyes to Hat. Weave in ends. ♦

lion

SIZES

Small [Medium; Large]

SUPPLIES

Worsted weight yarn in gold 425 yds [550; 610] and variegated brown-tone homespun yarn 25 yds plus small amount of black and white

F5/3.75mm, G6/4mm, H8/5mm and J10/6mm [G6/4mm, H8/5mm and J10/6mm; H8/5mm, I9/5.5mm, J10/6mm, and K10.5/6.5mm] crochet hooks or size needed to obtain gauge

2 gold animal eyes, 24mm

Wire cutters

Sewing needle and thread

Cardboard scrap

Stitch marker

Yarn needle

GAUGE

With J10/6mm hook and 2 strands of yarn held together:

5 rnds of sc = 3" diameter circle

HAT

With J10/6mm hook and 2 strands of gold yarn held together, make a magic ring, ch 1.

Rnd 1: 6 sc in ring, pull ring closed tight (6 sts).

Rnd 2: 2 sc in each st around. Place marker for beginning of rnd and move marker up as each rnd is completed (12 sts).

Rnd 3: *sc in next st, 2 sc in next st* 6 times (18 sts).

Rnd 4: *sc in next 2 sts, 2 sc in next st* 6 times (24 sts).

Rnd 5: *sc in next 3 sts, 2 sc in next st* 6 times (30 sts).

Rnd 6: *sc in next 4 sts, 2 sc in next st* 6 times (36 sts).

Rnd 7: *sc in next 5 sts, 2 sc in next st* 6 times (42 sts).

Rnd 8: *sc in next 6 sts, 2 sc in next st* 6 times (48 sts).

Rnd 9: *sc in next 7 sts, 2 sc in next st* 6 times (54 sts).

Rnd 10: *sc in next 8 sts, 2 sc in next st* 6 times (60 sts).

• FOR SIZE SMALL:

Rnds 11-25: sc in each st around. Fasten off.

• FOR SIZE MEDIUM:

Rnd 11: *sc in next 9 sts, 2 sc in next st* 6 times (66 sts).

Rnds 12-27: sc in each st around. Fasten off.

• FOR SIZE LARGE:

Rnd 11: *sc in next 9 sts, 2 sc in next st* 6 times (66 sts).

Rnd 12: *sc in next 10 sts, 2 sc in next st* 6 times (72 sts).

Rnds 13-29: sc in each st around. Fasten off.

SCARF (MAKE 2)

Mark position of Scarf (see page 14). Work Scarf into sts between markers, not including marked sts.

• **For size Small,** work in the 10 sts between each set of markers.

• **For size Medium,** work in the 12 sts between each set of markers.

• **For size Large,** work in the 14 sts between each set of markers.

Note: A chain 1 at the beginning of a row is for turning your work and does not count as a stitch.

Row 1: With J10/6mm hook and 2 strands of gold yarn held together, attach yarn in 1st st with sc, sc in each remaining st across. Place marker for beginning of row and move marker up as each row is completed.

Row 2: ch 1, turn, sc in each st across.

Rows 3-end: Repeat Row 2 until scarf is about 20" long.

EDGE TRIM

Using J10/6mm hook and 2 strands of gold yarn held together, attach yarn at center back of Hat with sc. Sc in each st around perimeter of Hat and Scarves making 3 sts in same st at lower corners of Scarves. Fasten off.

EAR (MAKE 2)

With hook size H8/5mm [J10/6mm: K10.5/6.5mm] and 2 strands of gold yarn held together, make a magic ring, ch 1.

Rnd 1: 6 sc in ring, pull ring closed tight (6 sts).

Rnd 2: 2 sc in each st around. Place marker for beginning of rnd and move marker up as each rnd is completed (12 sts).

Rnd 3: *sc in next st, 2 sc in next st* 6 times (18 sts).

Rnd 4: *sc in next 2 sts, 2 sc in next st* 6 times (24 sts).

Rnds 5-11: sc in each st around.

Fasten off with long tail.

NOSE

With G6/4mm [H8/5mm; I9/5.5mm] hook and a single strand of gold yarn, ch 9 loosely.

Note: A chain 1 at the beginning of a row is for turning your work and does not count as a stitch.

Row 1: sc in 2nd ch from hook and in each remaining ch across (8 sts).

Rows 2-10: ch 1, turn, sc in each st across; change to black yarn in last st (8 sts).

Row 11: ch 1, turn, sc2tog, sc in next 4 sts, sc2tog (6 sts).

Row 12: ch 1, turn, sc2tog, sc in next 2 sts, sc2tog (4 sts).

Row 13 ch 1, turn, sc2tog twice (2 sts).

Row 14: ch 1, turn, sc2tog (1 st).

Fasten off with long tail.

INNER EYE RIM (MAKE 2)

With H8/5mm hook and a single strand of black yarn, make a magic ring, ch 1.

Rnd 1: 8 sc in ring, pull ring closed almost tight (8 sts).

Rnd 2a: 2 sc in next 3 sts (6 sts).

Point: ch 2 and sc in 2nd ch from hook, sc in next st.

Rnd 2b: 2 sc in next 3 sts (6 sts).

Point: ch 2 and sc in 2nd ch from hook, sc in next st.

Sl st in next st. Fasten off with long tail.

OUTER EYE RIM (MAKE 2)

With J10/6mm hook and 2 strands of white yarn held together, make a magic ring, ch 1.

Rnd 1: 8 sc in ring, pull ring closed almost tight (8 sts).

Rnd 2a: 2 sc in next 3 sts (6 sts).

Point: ch 2 and sc in 2nd ch from hook, sc in next st.

Rnd 2b: 2 sc in next 3 sts (6 sts).

Point: ch 2 and sc in 2nd ch from hook, sc in next st.

Sl st in next st. Fasten off with long tail.

TOE PAD (MAKE 8)

This is worked around a foundation chain.

With hook size F5/3.75mm [G6/4mm; H8/5mm] and a single strand of black yarn, ch 4 loosely.

Rnd 1: starting in 2nd ch from hook, *sc in next 2 sts, 3 sc in next st* 2 times (10 sts).

St st in next st. Fasten off. Weave in ends.

HEEL PAD (MAKE 2)

With hook size F5/3.75mm [G6/4mm; H8/5mm] and a single strand of black yarn, ch 2.

Row 1: 3 sc in 2nd ch from hook.

Row 2: ch 1, turn, 2 sc in next 3 sts (6 sts).

Row 3: ch 1, turn, *sc in next st, 2 sc in next st* 3 times (9 sts).

Row 4: ch 1, turn, *sc in next 2 sts, 2 sc in next st* 3 times (12 sts).

Row 5: ch 1, turn, *sc in next 3 sts, 2 sc in next st* 3 times (15 sts).

Row 6: ch 1, turn, *sc in next 4 sts, 2 sc in next st* 3 times (18 sts).

Row 7: ch 1, do not turn, 5 dc in st at A (see below), sl st in B, 5 dc in C, sl st in D, 5 dc in E, sl st in F.

Fasten off. Weave in ends.

MANE

You will need many 6-inch pieces of variegated brown Homespun yarn to make the Mane. To quickly cut the strands, wrap yarn widthwise around a 3" x 9" piece of cardboard. On one side, insert scissors between cardboard and yarn—and cut.

Flatten Hat so that center front meets center back. With contrasting yarn and running stitch, sew a row of basting stitches along the crease—over top of Hat—starting and ending where Scarf meets Hat (see Fig. A).

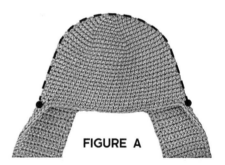

FIGURE A

Attach one 6" strand of Homespun yarn in each sc along baste line using Fringe technique (see page 16).

Flatten Ears and sew in place behind 1st row of fringe. Work 2 more rows of fringe: one in front and one in back of 1st row.

Fill in forehead area with 1 more row of fringe extending from mid-ear to mid-ear. Clip off any visible ends of basting stitches. Separate fibers in Mane strands with fingers for more fullness. Trim straggly ends.

ASSEMBLY

With a single strand of white yarn, embroider whiskers by making 1 stitch, about 2 1/2" long, for each whisker. Sew Nose to Hat. Stack Inner Eye Rims on Outer Eye Rims and sew together. Insert animal eyes through center and attach. Clip off excess post with wire cutters. Note: It can be difficult to push the washer portion of safety eyes onto the post when pushing through multiple layers of fabric. In this case, a socket wrench is a great aid. Choose a socket slightly smaller than the washer, position socket and press firmly. Otherwise, you can clip off posts and attach animal eyes with hot glue. Sew eyes to Hat. Sew Heel and Toe Pads to back side of Scarf ends with sewing needle and thread, taking shallow sts so sts don't show on front side (see photo below). Weave in ends. ◆

owl

SIZES

Small [Medium; Large]

SUPPLIES

Worsted weight yarn in golden-
brown 300 yds [385; 425];
gold 40 yds; dark brown
30 yds; plus small amount of
off-white, black and yellow

G6/4mm, H8/5mm and J10/6mm
[H8/5mm and J10/6mm;
I9/5.5mm, J10/6mm and
K10.5/6.5mm] crochet hooks
or size needed to obtain
gauge

2 yellow animal eyes, 24mm

Wire cutters

Stuffing

Stitch marker

Yarn needle

GAUGE

With J10/6mm hook and 2 strands
of yarn held together:

5 rnds of sc = 3" diameter circle

HAT

With J10/6mm hook and 2 strands
of golden-brown yarn held
together, make a magic ring, ch 1.

Rnd 1: 6 sc in ring, pull ring closed
tight (6 sts).

Rnd 2: 2 sc in each st around.
Place marker for beginning of rnd
and move marker up as each rnd
is completed (12 sts).

Rnd 3: *sc in next st, 2 sc in next
st* 6 times (18 sts).

Rnd 4: *sc in next 2 sts, 2 sc in
next st* 6 times (24 sts).

Rnd 5: *sc in next 3 sts, 2 sc in
next st* 6 times (30 sts).

Rnd 6: *sc in next 4 sts, 2 sc in
next st* 6 times (36 sts).

Rnd 7: *sc in next 5 sts, 2 sc in next
st* 6 times (42 sts).

Rnd 8: *sc in next 6 sts, 2 sc in
next st* 6 times (48 sts).

Rnd 9: *sc in next 7 sts, 2 sc in
next st* 6 times (54 sts).

Rnd 10: *sc in next 8 sts, 2 sc in
next st* 6 times (60 sts).

• FOR SIZE SMALL:

Rnds 11-25: sc in each st around.
Fasten off.

• FOR SIZE MEDIUM:

Rnd 11: *sc in next 9 sts, 2 sc in
next st* 6 times (66 sts).

Rnds 12-27: sc in each st around.
Fasten off.

• FOR SIZE LARGE:

Rnd 11: *sc in next 9 sts, 2 sc in
next st* 6 times (66 sts).

Rnd 12: *sc in next 10 sts, 2 sc in
next st* 6 times (72 sts).

Rnds 13-29: sc in each st around.
Fasten off.

EAR FLAP (MAKE 2)

Mark position of Ear Flaps (see
page 14). Work Ear Flaps into sts
between markers, not including
the marked sts.

• **For size Small,** work in the 10 sts
between each set of markers.

• **For size Medium,** work in the 12
sts between each set of markers.

• **For size Large,** work in the 14
sts between each set of markers.

Note: A chain 1 at the beginning of
a row is for turning your work and
does not count as a stitch.

Row 1: With J10/6mm hook and
2 strands of golden-brown yarn
held together, attach yarn in 1st
st with sc, sc in each remaining st
across. Place marker for beginning
of row and move marker up as
each row is completed.

Row 2: ch 1, turn, skip next st, sc in
each remaining st across.

Rows 3-end: Repeat Row 2 until
only 3 sc remain, ch 1, turn, insert

hook in each st and pull up a loop. You will have 4 loops on hook. Yarn over and pull through all 4 loops.

Fasten off. Weave in ends.

EDGE TRIM

With J10/6mm hook and 2 strands of yarn held together, sc in each st around perimeter of Hat making 3 sts in same st at tip of each Ear Flap. Use off-white yarn across front and golden-brown yarn around Ear Flaps and back. Fasten off.

TWISTED CORD TIE (MAKE 2)

Cut eight 54" strands of gold yarn and eight 54" strands of dark brown yarn. Follow instructions on page 15.

EYE RIM (MAKE 2)

With G6/4mm [H8/5mm; I9/5.5mm] hook and a single strand of black yarn, make a magic ring, ch 1.

Rnd 1: 6 sc in ring, pull ring closed almost tight (6 sts).

Rnd 2: 2 sc in each st around. Place marker for beginning of rnd and move marker up as each rnd is completed (12 sts).

Rnd 3: *sc in next st, 2 sc in next st* 6 times; change to off-white yarn in last st (18 sts).

Rnd 4: *sc in next 2 sts, 2 sc in next st* 6 times; change to gold yarn in last st (24 sts).

Rnd 5: *sc in next 3 sts, 2 sc in next st* 6 times (30 sts).

Rnd 6: *sc in next 4 sts, 2 sc in next st* 6 times (36 sts).

Rnd 7: *sc in next 5 sts, 2 sc in next st* 6 times (42 sts).

Rnd 8: *sc in next 6 sts, 2 sc in next st* 6 times; change to dark brown yarn in last st (48 sts).

Rnd 9: *sc in next 7 sts, 2 sc in next st* 6 times (54 sts).

Sl st in next st. Fasten off with long tail.

TOP TRIANGLE

The triangle is created by decreasing at the beginning and end of each row.

With hook size H8/5mm [J10/6mm; K10.5/6.5mm] and 2 strands of golden-brown yarn held together, ch 45 loosely.

Note: A chain 1 at the beginning of a row is for turning your work and does not count as a stitch.

Row 1: starting in 2nd ch from hook, sc2tog, sc in each ch across until 2 ch remain, sc2tog.

Rows 2-end: ch 1, turn, sc2tog, sc in each st across until 2 sts remain, sc2tog. Continue working rows in this manner until 1 st remains.

Fasten off.

EAR TRIANGLE (MAKE 2)

With hook size H8/5mm [J10/6mm; K10.5/6.5mm] and 2 strands of golden-brown yarn held together, ch 9 loosely.

Note: A chain 1 at the beginning of a row is for turning your work and does not count as a stitch.

Row 1: starting in 2nd ch from hook, sc in each ch across (8 sts).

Row 2: ch 1, turn, sc2tog, sc in next 4 sts, sc2tog (6 sts).

Row 3: ch 1, turn, sc in each st across (6 sts).

Row 4: ch 1, turn, sc2tog, sc in next 2 sts, sc2tog (4 sts).

Row 5: ch 1, turn, sc in each st across (4 sts).

Row 6: ch 1, turn, sc2tog twice (2 sts).

Row 7: ch 1, turn, sc2tog (1 st).

Fasten off. With wrong sides together, pin Ear Triangles to upper tips of Top Triangle (see X and Y on Fig. A).

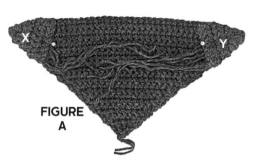

FIGURE A

Sc around perimeter of Top Triangle using off-white yarn for 3" on each side of center front, golden-brown yarn for the remainder and making 3 sts in same st at each corner. Note: At Ear Triangles, crochet through all layers so that Ear Triangles become attached.

TUFT (MAKE 2)

Cut three 8-inch strands of gold and three 8-inch strands of dark brown yarn. Lay strands together and attach to tip "X" of Top Triangle using Fringe technique (see page 16). Trim to 1 inch. Repeat for tip "Y".

BEAK

With G6/4mm [H8/5mm; I9/5.5mm] hook and a single strand of yellow yarn, make a magic ring, ch 1.

Rnd 1: 6 sc in ring, pull ring closed tight (6 sts).

Rnd 2: 2 sc in each st around. Place marker for beginning of rnd and move marker up as each rnd is completed (12 sts).

Rnd 3: *sc in next st, 2 sc in next st* 6 times (18 sts).

Rnd 4: *sc in next 2 sts, 2 sc in next st* 6 times (24 sts).

Fasten off.

With wrong side up, fold sides to the center (see A). Now fold in half lengthwise (see B). Sew to hold in position (see C).

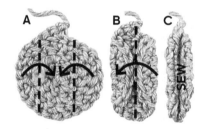

ASSEMBLY

Attach animal eyes to center of Eye Rims. Trim off excess post with wire cutters. Pin Eye Rims to Hat placing the uneven jog where color was changed so that jog will be hidden by Top Triangle. Sew Eye Rims to Hat. Sew Beak to Hat. Stuff Ear Triangles (you can also tuck any straggly yarn tails inside). Sew Top Triangle to Hat: when doing this, sew open edge of Ear Triangles to Hat and leave tips of Top Triangle detached. Weave in ends. ♦

tiger

In working the striped pieces of the Tiger, carry the yarn not in use along the side. This means to leave the color you are currently not using at the side of your work without cutting it.

SIZES

Small [Medium; Large]

SUPPLIES

Worsted weight yarn in orange 220 yds [280; 310] and black 260 yds [330; 365] plus small amount of white

Size G6/4mm, H8/5mm and J10/6mm [H8/5mm and J10/6mm; H8/5mm, I9/5.5mm, J10/6mm, and K10.5/6.5mm] crochet hooks or size needed to obtain gauge

2 yellow animal eyes, 24mm

Wire cutters

Stitch marker

Yarn needle

GAUGE

With J10/6mm hook and 2 strands of yarn held together:

5 rnds of sc = 3" diameter circle

HAT

With J10/6mm hook and 2 strands of orange yarn held together, make a magic ring, ch 1.

• FOR SIZE SMALL:

Rnd 1: 6 sc in ring, pull ring closed tight (6 sts).

Rnd 2: 2 sc in each st around; change to black yarn in last st. Place marker for beginning of rnd and move marker up as each rnd is completed (12 sts).

Rnd 3: *sc in next st, 2 sc in next st* 6 times (18 sts).

Rnd 4: *sc in next 2 sts, 2 sc in next st* 6 times; change to orange yarn in last st (24 sts).

Rnd 5: *sc in next 3 sts, 2 sc in next st* 6 times (30 sts).

Rnd 6: *sc in next 4 sts, 2 sc in next st* 6 times (36 sts).

Rnd 7: *sc in next 5 sts, 2 sc in next st* 6 times; change to black yarn in last st (42 sts).

Rnd 8: *sc in next 6 sts, 2 sc in next st* 6 times; change to orange yarn in last st (48 sts).

Rnd 9: *sc in next 7 sts, 2 sc in next st* 6 times (54 sts).

Rnd 10: *sc in next 8 sts, 2 sc in next st* 6 times (60 sts).

Rnd 11: sc in each st around; change to black yarn in last st.

Rnds 12-13: sc in each st around; change to orange yarn in last st.

Rnds 14-16: sc in each st around; change to black yarn in last st.

Rnd 17: sc in each st around; change to orange yarn in last st.

Rnds 18-20: sc in each st around; change to black yarn in last st.

Rnds 21-22: sc in each st around; change to orange yarn in last st.

Rnds 23-25: sc in each st around. Fasten off.

• FOR SIZE MEDIUM:

Rnd 1: 6 sc in ring, pull ring closed tight (6 sts).

Rnd 2: 2 sc in each st around. Place marker for beginning of rnd and move marker up as each rnd is completed (12 sts).

Rnd 3: *sc in next st, 2 sc in next st* 6 times (18 sts).

Rnd 4: *sc in next 2 sts, 2 sc in next st* 6 times; change to black yarn in last st (24 sts).

Rnd 5: *sc in next 3 sts, 2 sc in next st* 6 times (30 sts).

Rnd 6: *sc in next 4 sts, 2 sc in next st* 6 times; change to orange yarn in last st (36 sts).

Rnd 7: *sc in next 5 sts, 2 sc in next st* 6 times (42 sts).

Rnd 8: *sc in next 6 sts, 2 sc in next st* 6 times (48 sts).

Rnd 9: *sc in next 7 sts, 2 sc in next st* 6 times; change to black yarn in last st (54 sts).

Rnd 10: *sc in next 8 sts, 2 sc in next st* 6 times; change to orange yarn in last st (60 sts).

Rnd 11: *sc in next 9 sts, 2 sc in next st* 6 times (66 sts).

Rnds 12-13: sc in each st around; change to black yarn in last st.

Rnds 14-15: sc in each st around; change to orange yarn in last st.

Rnds 16-18: sc in each st around; change to black yarn in last st.

Rnds 19: sc in each st around; change to orange yarn in last st.

Rnds 20-22: sc in each st around; change to black yarn in last st.

Rnds 23-24: sc in each st around; change to orange yarn in last st.

Rnds 25-27: sc in each st around. Fasten off.

• FOR SIZE LARGE:

Rnd 1: 6 sc in ring, pull ring closed tight (6 sts).

Rnd 2: 2 sc in each st around; change to black yarn in last st.

Place marker for beginning of rnd and move marker up as each rnd is completed (12 sts).

Rnd 3: *sc in next st, 2 sc in next st* 6 times; change to orange yarn in last st (18 sts).

Rnd 4: *sc in next 2 sts, 2 sc in next st* 6 times (24 sts).

Rnd 5: *sc in next 3 sts, 2 sc in next st* 6 times (30 sts).

Rnd 6: *sc in next 4 sts, 2 sc in next st* 6 times; change to black yarn in last st (36 sts).

Rnd 7: *sc in next 5 sts, 2 sc in next st* 6 times (42 sts).

Rnd 8: *sc in next 6 sts, 2 sc in next st* 6 times; change to orange yarn in last st (48 sts).

Rnd 9: *sc in next 7 sts, 2 sc in next st* 6 times (54 sts).

Rnd 10: *sc in next 8 sts, 2 sc in next st* 6 times (60 sts).

Rnd 11: *sc in next 9 sts, 2 sc in next st* 6 times; change to black yarn in last st (66 sts).

Rnd 12: *sc in next 10 sts, 2 sc in next st* 6 times; change to orange yarn in last st (72 sts).

Rnds 13-15: sc in each st around; change to black yarn in last st.

Rnds 16-17: sc in each st around; change to orange yarn in last st..

Rnds 18-20: sc in each st around; change to black yarn in last st.

Rnd 21: sc in each st around; change to orange yarn in last st..

Rnds 22-24: sc in each st around; change to black yarn in last st.

Rnds 25-26: sc in each st around; change to orange yarn in last st..

Rnds 27-29: sc in each st around. Fasten off.

SCARF (MAKE 2)

Mark position of Scarf (see page 14). Work Scarf into sts between markers, not including marked sts.

• **For size Small,** work in the 10 sts between each set of markers.

• **For size Medium,** work in the 12 sts between each set of markers.

• **For size Large,** work in the 14 sts between each set of markers.

Note: A chain 1 at the beginning of a row is for turning your work and does not count as a stitch.

The Scarf is worked in rows following the same stripe pattern as the Hat: alternate 1 then 2 rows of black with 3 rows of orange. Start with 1 row of black.

Row 1: With J10/6mm hook and 2 strands of yarn held together, attach yarn in 1st st with sc, sc in each remaining st across. Place marker for beginning of row and move marker up as each row is completed.

Row 2: ch 1, turn, sc in each st across.

Rows 3-end: Repeat Row 2 until scarf is about 20" long, ending with 3 rows of orange.

Note: Carry the yarn not in use along the side. When a stripe contains 1 or 3 rows, you will also need to carry the previous color across the row (and crochet over it) to have it at the proper side when it is needed again.

EDGE TRIM

Using J10/6mm hook and 2 strands of black yarn held together, attach yarn at center back of Hat with sc. Sc in each st around perimeter of Hat and Scarves making 3 sts in same st at lower corners of Scarves. Fasten off.

INNER EAR (MAKE 2)

With G6/4mm [H8/5mm; I9/5.5mm] hook and a single strand of white yarn, ch 2.

Note: A chain 1 at the beginning of a row is for turning your work and does not count as a stitch.

Row 1: 5 sc in 2nd ch from hook (5 sts).

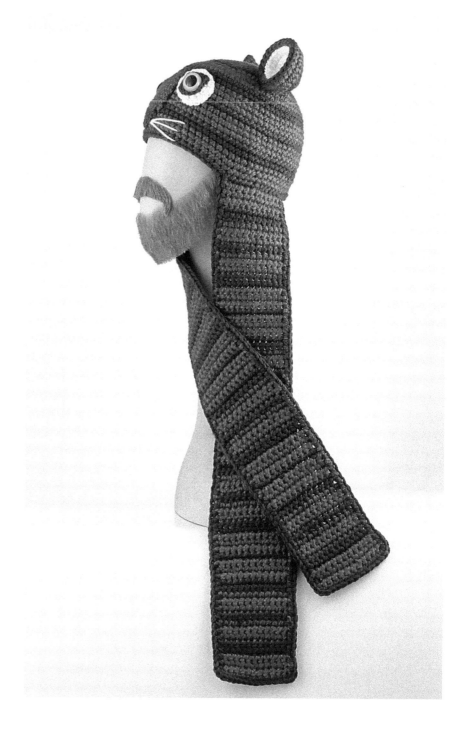

Row 2: ch 1, turn, 2 sc in each st across (10 sts).

Row 3: ch 1, turn *sc in next st, 2 sc in next st* 5 times (15 sts).

Row 4: ch 1, turn *sc in next 2 sts, 2 sc in next st* 5 times (20 sts).

Row 5: ch 1, turn *sc in next 3 sts, 2 sc in next st* 5 times (25 sts).

Rows 6-8: ch 1, turn, sc in each st across.

Fasten off with long tail.

OUTER EAR (MAKE 2)

With hook size H8/5mm [J10/6mm; K10.5/6.5mm] and 2 strands of orange yarn held together, ch 2.

Note: A chain 1 at the beginning of a row is for turning your work and does not count as a stitch.

Row 1: 5 sc in 2nd ch from hook (5 sts).

Row 2: ch 1, turn, 2 sc in each st across; change to black yarn in last st (10 sts).

Row 3: ch 1, turn *sc in next st, 2 sc in next st* 5 times (15 sts).

Row 4: ch 1, turn *sc in next 2 sts, 2 sc in next st* 5 times; change to orange yarn in last st (20 sts).

Row 5: ch 1, turn *sc in next 3 sts, 2 sc in next st* 5 times (25 sts).

Row 6: ch 1, turn, sc in each st across.

Row 7: ch 1, turn, sc in each st across; change to black yarn in last st.

Row 8: ch 1, turn, sl st in each st across.

Fasten off with long tail.

EYE RIM (MAKE 2)

With H8/5mm hook and a single strand of black yarn, make a magic ring, ch 1.

Rnd 1: 8 sc in ring, pull ring closed almost tight (8 sts).

Rnd 2a: 2 sc in next 3 sts (6 sts).

Point: ch 2 and sc in 2nd ch from hook, sc in next st.

Rnd 2b: 2 sc in next 3 sts (6 sts).

Point: ch 2 and sc in 2nd ch from hook, sc in next st.

Sl st in next st. Fasten off with long tail.

OUTER EYE (MAKE 2)

With H8/5mm hook and a single strand of white yarn, make a magic ring, ch 1.

Rnd 1: 6 sc in ring, pull ring closed almost tight (6 sts).

Rnd 2: 2 sc in each st around. Place marker for beginning of rnd and move marker up as each rnd is completed (12 sts).

Rnd 3: *sc in next st, 2 sc in next st* 6 times (18 sts).

Rnd 4: *2 sc in next st, sc in next 2 sts* 6 times (24 sts).

Sl st in next st. Fasten off with long tail.

NOSE

With G6/4mm [H8/5mm; I9/5.5mm] hook and a single strand of orange yarn, ch 9 loosely.

Note: A chain 1 at the beginning of a row is for turning your work and does not count as a stitch.

Row 1: sc in 2nd ch from hook and in each remaining ch across (8 sts).

Rows 2-10: ch 1, turn, sc in each st across; change to black yarn in last st (8 sts).

Row 11: ch 1, turn, sc2tog, sc in next 4 sts, sc2tog (6 sts).

Row 12: ch 1, turn, sc2tog, sc in next 2 sts, sc2tog (4 sts).

Row 13 ch 1, turn, sc2tog twice (2 sts).

Row 14: ch 1, turn, sc2tog (1 st).

Fasten off with long tail.

ASSEMBLY

With a single strand of white yarn, embroider whiskers by making 1 stitch, about 2 1/2" long, for each whisker. Sew Nose to Hat. Stack Eye Rims on Outer Eyes. Insert animal eyes through the center and attach. Trim off excess post with wire cutters. Sew Eye Rims to Outer Eyes. Sew Eyes to Hat. Stack Inner Ears on Outer Ears wrong sides together so that starting tails meet and straight sides align. Trim and tuck excess ends of yarn between the layers. Whip stitch pieces together along straight sides and sew together along curved edge catching only wrong-side loops so that sts don't show on outside. Fold Ears so that straight sides meet and sew together (this will make a cup shape). Temporarily flatten Ears along seam and sew in place to Hat along both sides of seamline. Weave in ends. ♦

penguin

SIZES

Small [Medium; Large]

SUPPLIES

Worsted weight yarn in black 200 yds [250; 275]; white 60 yds and orange 50 yds

G6/4mm and J10/6mm [H8/5mm and J10/6mm; I9/5.5mm, and J10/6mm] crochet hooks or size needed to obtain gauge

2 blue animal eyes, 24mm

Wire cutters

Stuffing

Cardboard scrap

Sewing needle and thread

Stitch marker

Yarn needle

GAUGE

With J10/6mm hook and 2 strands of yarn held together:

5 rnds of sc = 3" diameter circle

HAT

With J10/6mm hook and 2 strands of black yarn held together, make a magic ring, ch 1.

Rnd 1: 6 sc in ring, pull ring closed tight (6 sts).

Rnd 2: 2 sc in each st around. Place marker for beginning of rnd and move marker up as each rnd is completed (12 sts).

Rnd 3: *sc in next st, 2 sc in next st* 6 times (18 sts).

Rnd 4: *sc in next 2 sts, 2 sc in next st* 6 times (24 sts).

Rnd 5: *sc in next 3 sts, 2 sc in next st* 6 times (30 sts).

Rnd 6: *sc in next 4 sts, 2 sc in next st* 6 times (36 sts).

Rnd 7: *sc in next 5 sts, 2 sc in next st* 6 times (42 sts).

Rnd 8: *sc in next 6 sts, 2 sc in next st* 6 times (48 sts).

Rnd 9: *sc in next 7 sts, 2 sc in next st* 6 times (54 sts).

Rnd 10: *sc in next 8 sts, 2 sc in next st* 6 times (60 sts).

• FOR SIZE SMALL:

Rnds 11-25: sc in each st around. Fasten off.

• FOR SIZE MEDIUM:

Rnd 11: *sc in next 9 sts, 2 sc in next st* 6 times (66 sts).

Rnds 12-27: sc in each st around. Fasten off.

• FOR SIZE LARGE:

Rnd 11: *sc in next 9 sts, 2 sc in next st* 6 times (66 sts).

Rnd 12: *sc in next 10 sts, 2 sc in next st* 6 times (72 sts).

Rnds 13-29: sc in each st around. Fasten off.

EAR FLAP (MAKE 2)

Mark position of Ear Flaps (see page 14). Work Ear Flaps into sts between markers, not including the marked sts.

• **For size Small,** work in the 10 sts between each set of markers.

• **For size Medium,** work in the 12 sts between each set of markers.

• **For size Large,** work in the 14 sts between each set of markers.

Note: A chain 1 at the beginning of a row is for turning your work and does not count as a stitch.

Row 1: With J10/6mm hook and 2 strands of black yarn held together, attach yarn in 1st st with sc, sc in each remaining st across. Place marker for beginning of row and move marker up as each row is completed.

Row 2: ch 1, turn, skip next st, sc in each remaining st across.

Rows 3-end: Repeat Row 2 until only 3 sc remain, ch 1, turn, insert

hook in each st and pull up a loop. You will have 4 loops on hook. Yarn over and pull through all 4 loops.

Fasten off. Weave in ends.

EDGE TRIM

Using J10/6mm hook and 2 strands of white yarn held together, attach yarn at center back of Hat with sc. Sc in each st around perimeter of Hat making 3 sts in same st at tip of each Ear Flap. Fasten off.

UPPER FACE (MAKE 2)

With G6/4mm [H8/5mm; I9/5.5mm] hook and a single strand of white yarn, ch 2.

Note: A chain 1 at the beginning of a row is for turning your work and does not count as a stitch.

Row 1: 3 sc in 2nd ch from hook.

Row 2: ch 1, turn, 2 sc in next 3 sts (6 sts).

Row 3: ch 1, turn, *sc in next st, 2 sc in next st* 3 times (9 sts).

Row 4: ch 1, turn, *sc in next 2 sts, 2 sc in next st* 3 times (12 sts).

Row 5: ch 1, turn, *sc in next 3 sts, 2 sc in next st* 3 times (15 sts).

Row 6: ch 1, turn, *sc in next 4 sts, 2 sc in next st* 3 times (18 sts).

Row 7: ch 1, turn, *sc in next 5 sts, 2 sc in next st* 3 times (21 sts).

Fasten off with long tail.

LOWER FACE

With G6/4mm [H8/5mm; I9/5.5mm] hook and a single strand of white yarn, ch 29 loosely.

Note: A chain 1 at the beginning of a row is for turning your work and does not count as a stitch.

Row 1: sc in 2nd ch from hook and in each remaining ch across (28 sts).

Rows 2-11: ch 1, turn, sc in each st across (28 sts).

Fasten off with long tail. Sew Upper Face pieces to Lower Face. Single crochet around entire perimeter. Fasten off.

BEAK

With G6/4mm [H8/5mm; I9/5.5mm] hook and a single strand of orange yarn, make a magic ring, ch 1.

Rnd 1: 6 sc in ring, pull ring closed tight (6 sts).

Rnd 2: *sc in next st, 2 sc in next st* 3 times (9 sts).

Rnd 3: *sc in next 2 sts, 2 sc in next st* 3 times (12 sts).

Rnd 4: *sc in next 3 sts, 2 sc in next st* 3 times (15 sts).

Rnd 5: *sc in next 4 sts, 2 sc in next st* 3 times (18 sts).

Rnd 6: *sc in next 5 sts, 2 sc in next st* 3 times (21 sts).

Rnd 7: *sc in next 6 sts, 2 sc in next st* 3 times (24 sts).

Rnd 8: *sc in next 7 sts, 2 sc in next st* 3 times (27 sts).

Rnd 9: *sc in next 8 sts, 2 sc in next st* 3 times (30 sts).

Rnd 10: *sc in next 9 sts, 2 sc in next st* 3 times (33 sts).

Rnd 11: *sc in next 10 sts, 2 sc in next st* 3 times (36 sts).

Sl st in next st. Fasten off with long tail.

BEAKLINE

With G6/4mm [H8/5mm; I9/5.5mm] hook and a single strand of orange yarn, ch tightly until chain is long enough to reach over Beak. Fasten off.

TASSELS (MAKE 2)

Cut a 5" x 10" piece of cardboard. Wrap orange yarn lengthwise around cardboard 13 times. Carefully slide yarn off cardboard. Using 2 strands of white yarn, about 18" long, tie bundle together tightly around the middle. Wrap white yarn to other side and tie tightly again! Cut loops open. Untwist orange yarn strands and separate the plies. Trim ends to 3".

ASSEMBLY

Attach animal eyes to Face and clip off excess post with wire cutters. Sew Face to Hat. Stuff Beak lightly and pin to Hat: notice how Beak has 3 points on perimeter and position 1 point at top center. Sew Beak to Hat, pausing to pack in more stuffing when you have about an inch left to sew. Pin Beakline in position across center of Beak and sew in place with sewing needle and thread. Tie Tassels to Ear Flaps. Weave in ends. ◆

shark

SIZES

Small [Medium; Large]

SUPPLIES

Worsted weight yarn in gray 520 yds [670; 740] plus small amount of white and red

Size H8/5mm and J10/6mm [H8/5mm and J10/6mm; H8/5mm, J10/6mm and K10.5/6.5mm] crochet hooks or size needed to obtain gauge

2 black animal eyes, 24mm

Stuffing

Wire cutters

Stitch marker

Yarn needle

GAUGE

With J10/6mm hook and 2 strands of yarn held together:

5 rnds of sc = 3" diameter circle

HAT

With J10/6mm hook and 2 strands of gray yarn held together, make a magic ring, ch 1.

Rnd 1: 6 sc in ring, pull ring closed tight (6 sts).

Rnd 2: 2 sc in each st around.

Place marker for beginning of rnd and move marker up as each rnd is completed (12 sts).

Rnd 3: sc in each st around.

Rnd 4: sc in next 11 sts, 2 sc in next st (13 sts).

Rnd 5: sc in next 12 sts, 2 sc in next st (14 sts).

Rnd 6: sc in next 13 sts, 2 sc in next st (15 sts).

Rnd 7: sc in next 14 sts, 2 sc in next st (16 sts).

Rnd 8: sc in next 15 sts, 2 sc in next st (17 sts).

Rnd 9: sc in next 16 sts, 2 sc in next st (18 sts).

Rnds 10-13: sc in each st around.

Rnd 14: *sc in next 2 sts, 2 sc in next st* 6 times (24 sts).

Rnds 15-19: sc in each st around.

Rnd 20: *sc in next 3 sts, 2 sc in next st* 6 times (30 sts).

Rnds 21-25: sc in each st around.

Rnd 26: *sc in next 4 sts, 2 sc in next st* 6 times (36 sts).

Rnds 27-32: sc in each st around.

Rnd 33: *sc in next 5 sts, 2 sc in next st* 6 times (42 sts).

Rnds 34-39: sc in each st around.

Rnd 40: *sc in next 6 sts, 2 sc in next st* 6 times (48 sts).

Rnds 41-46: sc in each st around.

Rnd 47: *sc in next 7 sts, 2 sc in next st* 6 times (54 sts).

Rnds 48-53: sc in each st around.

Rnd 54: *sc in next 8 sts, 2 sc in next st* 6 times (60 sts).

Rnds 55-60: sc in each st around.

• FOR SIZE SMALL:

Rnds 61-75: sc in each st around. Fasten off.

• FOR SIZE MEDIUM:

Rnd 61: *sc in next 9 sts, 2 sc in next st* 6 times (66 sts).

Rnds 62-77: sc in each st around. Fasten off.

• FOR SIZE LARGE:

Rnd 61: *sc in next 9 sts, 2 sc in next st* 6 times (66 sts).

Rnd 62: *sc in next 10 sts, 2 sc in next st* 6 times (72 sts).

Rnds 63-79: sc in each st around. Fasten off.

EAR FLAP (MAKE 2)

Mark position of Ear Flaps (see page 14). Work Ear Flaps into sts between markers, not including the marked sts.

• **For size Small,** work in the 10 sts between each set of markers.

• **For size Medium,** work in the 12 sts between each set of markers.

• **For size Large,** work in the 14 sts between each set of markers.

Note: A chain 1 at the beginning of a row is for turning your work and does not count as a stitch.

Row 1: With J10/6mm hook and 2 strands of gray yarn held together, attach yarn in 1st st with sc, sc in each remaining st across. Place marker for beginning of row and move marker up as each row is completed.

Row 2: ch 1, turn, skip next st, sc in each remaining st across.

Rows 3-end: Repeat Row 2 until only 3 sc remain, ch 1, turn, insert hook in each st and pull up a loop. You will have 4 loops on hook. Yarn over and pull through all 4 loops. Fasten off. Weave in ends.

EDGE TRIM

With J10/6mm hook and 2 strands of yarn held together, crochet around opening edge of Hat using red across front and back, and gray around Ear Flaps, making 3 sts in same st at tip of each Ear Flap. Fasten off.

TEETH

With J10/6mm hook and 2 strands of white yarn held together, fasten on and sl st loosely in back loop of each red st across front of Hat. This creates the foundation row for your Teeth. Turn, *ch 5, sl st in 2nd ch from hook, sc in next ch, hdc in next ch, dc in last ch, **skip 2 sts**, sl st loosely in front loop of next 2 sts* across foundation row. Note: You should end with a complete tooth aligned with the beginning of the foundation row. If necessary, adjust "skip 2 sts" (see bold text above) to "skip 1 st" or "skip 3 sts" as needed for a good fit. Fasten off. Repeat on back of Hat.

TOP FIN

With hook size H8/5mm [J10/6mm; K10.5/6.5mm] and 2 strands of gray yarn held together, make a magic ring, ch 1.

Rnd 1: 6 sc in ring, pull ring closed tight (6 sts).

Rnd 2: *sc in next st, 2 sc in next st* 3 times. Place marker for beginning of rnd and move marker up as each rnd is completed (9 sts).

Rnd 3: sc in each st around.

Rnd 4: *sc in next 2 sts, 2 sc in next st* 3 times (12 sts).

Rnd 5: sc in each st around.

Rnd 6: *sc in next 3 sts, 2 sc in next st* 3 times (15 sts).

Rnd 7: sc in each st around.

Rnd 8: *sc in next 4 sts, 2 sc in next st* 3 times (18 sts).

Rnd 9: sc in each st around.

Rnd 10: *sc in next 5 sts, 2 sc in next st* 3 times (21 sts).

Rnd 11: sc in each st around.

Rnd 12: *sc in next 6 sts, 2 sc in next st* 3 times (24 sts).

Fasten off with long tail. Using yarn needle, run long tail through stitches from base of long tail to tip of Fin, passing through the actual stitches. Pull long tail like a drawstring to shape Fin into a curve, knot to hold shape, and run needle back through Fin to opening edge. Note: A small v-shaped notch may form in opening edge of Fin at base of drawstring. If so, close it up with a stitch or two.

TOP FIN

TAIL FIN (MAKE 2)

With hook size H8/5mm [J10/6mm; K10.5/6.5mm] and 2 strands of gray yarn held together, make a magic ring, ch 1.

Rnd 1: 4 sc in ring, pull ring closed tight (4 sts).

Rnd 2: 2 sc in each st around. Place marker for beginning of rnd and move marker up as each rnd is completed (8 sts).

Rnd 3: *sc in next st, 2 sc in next st* 4 times (12 sts).

Rnd 4: sc in each st around.

Rnd 5: sc in next 11 sts, 2 sc in next st (13 sts).

Rnd 6: sc in next 12 sts, 2 sc in next st (14 sts).

Rnd 7: sc in next 13 sts, 2 sc in next st (15 sts).

Rnd 8: sc in next 14 sts, 2 sc in next st (16 sts).

Rnd 9: sc in next 15 sts, 2 sc in next st (17 sts).

Rnd 10: sc in next 16 sts, 2 sc in next st (18 sts).

Rnds 11-14: sc in each st around.

Rnd 15: *sc in next 2 sts, 2 sc in next st* 6 times (24 sts).

Rnd 16: sc in each st around.

Fasten off with long tail.

TAIL FINS

EYE RIM (MAKE 2)

With H8/5mm hook and a single strand of gray yarn, make a magic ring, ch 1.

Rnd 1: 6 sc in ring, pull ring closed almost tight (6 sts).

Rnd 2: 2 sc in each st around. Place marker for beginning of rnd and move marker up as each rnd is completed (12 sts).

Rnd 3: *sc in next st, 2 sc in next st* 6 times (18 sts).

Fasten off with long tail.

ASSEMBLY

Stuff Top Fin lightly and sew to top of Hat. Flatten Tail Fins, shape into a slight curve and sew to tip of Hat with curves facing inward (see photo).

Attach animal eyes to center of Eye Rims. Clip off excess post with wire cutters. Sew Eyes to Hat. Weave in ends. ♦

dog

SIZES

Small [Medium; Large]

SUPPLIES

Worsted weight yarn in tan 260 yds [330; 350]; brown 65 yds and small amount of black

G6/4mm, H8/5mm and J10/6mm [G6/4mm and J10/6mm; G6/4mm, J10/6mm and K10.5/6.5mm] crochet hooks or size needed to obtain gauge

2 black animal eyes, 24mm (or substitute black buttons)

Hot glue gun (high temperature) and glue stick

Cardboard scraps

Wire cutters

Stuffing

Stitch marker

Yarn needle

GAUGE

With J10/6mm hook and 2 strands of yarn held together:

5 rnds of sc = 3" diameter circle

HAT

With J10/6mm hook and 2 strands of tan yarn held together, make a magic ring, ch 1.

Rnd 1: 6 sc in ring, pull ring closed tight (6 sts).

Rnd 2: 2 sc in each st around. Place marker for beginning of rnd and move marker up as each rnd is completed (12 sts).

Rnd 3: *sc in next st, 2 sc in next st* 6 times (18 sts).

Rnd 4: *sc in next 2 sts, 2 sc in next st* 6 times (24 sts).

Rnd 5: *sc in next 3 sts, 2 sc in next st* 6 times (30 sts).

Rnd 6: *sc in next 4 sts, 2 sc in next st* 6 times (36 sts).

Rnd 7: *sc in next 5 sts, 2 sc in next st* 6 times (42 sts).

Rnd 8: *sc in next 6 sts, 2 sc in next st* 6 times (48 sts).

Rnd 9: *sc in next 7 sts, 2 sc in next st* 6 times (54 sts).

Rnd 10: *sc in next 8 sts, 2 sc in next st* 6 times (60 sts).

• **FOR SIZE SMALL:**

Rnds 11-25: sc in each st around. Fasten off.

• **FOR SIZE MEDIUM:**

Rnd 11: *sc in next 9 sts, 2 sc in next st* 6 times (66 sts).

Rnds 12-27: sc in each st around. Fasten off.

• **FOR SIZE LARGE:**

Rnd 11: *sc in next 9 sts, 2 sc in next st* 6 times (66 sts).

Rnd 12: *sc in next 10 sts, 2 sc in next st* 6 times (72 sts).

Rnds 13-29: sc in each st around. Fasten off.

EAR FLAP (MAKE 2)

Mark position of Ear Flaps (see page 14). Work Ear Flaps into sts between markers, not including the marked sts.

• **For size Small,** work in the 10 sts between each set of markers.

• **For size Medium,** work in the 12 sts between each set of markers.

• **For size Large,** work in the 14 sts between each set of markers.

Note: A chain 1 at the beginning of a row is for turning your work and does not count as a stitch.

Row 1: With J10/6mm hook and 2 strands of tan yarn held together, attach yarn in 1st st with sc, sc in each remaining st across. Place marker for beginning of row and move marker up as each row is completed.

Row 2: ch 1, turn, skip next st, sc in each remaining st across.

Rows 3-end: Repeat Row 2 until only 3 sc remain, ch 1, turn, insert

hook in each st and pull up a loop. You will have 4 loops on hook. Yarn over and pull through all 4 loops. Fasten off. Weave in ends.

EDGE TRIM

Using J10/6mm hook and 2 strands of brown yarn held together, attach yarn at center back of Hat with sc. Sc in each st around perimeter of Hat making 3 sts in same st at tip of each Ear Flap. Fasten off.

TWISTED CORD TIE (MAKE 2)

Cut eight 54" strands of tan yarn and eight 54" strands of brown yarn. Follow instructions page 15.

NOSE

With G6/4mm hook and a single strand of black yarn, make a magic ring, ch 1.

Rnd 1: 6 sc in ring, pull ring closed tight (6 sts).

Rnd 2: 2 sc in each st around. Place marker for beginning of rnd and move marker up as each rnd is completed (12 sts).

Rnd 3: sc in each st around.

Rnd 4: sc2tog 6 times (6 sts).

Fasten off with long tail. Pack in stuffing with eraser end of pencil. Sew opening shut.

EAR (MAKE 2)

Note: A chair back that is approximately 20" across can be substituted for cardboard to wrap the ears.

Cut a rectangle of cardboard measuring 5" x 20". With tan and brown yarn held together, wrap yarn lengthwise around cardboard 10 times. Carefully slide yarn off cardboard. Using 2 strands of matching yarn, tie bundle together tightly around the middle. Cut loops open.

SNOUT

With hook size H8/5mm [J10/6mm; K10.5/6.5mm] and 2 strands of tan yarn held together, make a magic ring, ch 1.

Rnd 1: 6 sc in ring, pull ring closed tight (6 sts).

Rnd 2: 2 sc in each st around. Place marker for beginning of rnd and move marker up as each rnd is completed (12 sts).

Rnd 3: *sc in next st, 2 sc in next st* 6 times (18 sts).

Rnd 4: *sc in next 2 sts, 2 sc in next st* 6 times (24 sts).

Rnds 5-7: sc in each st around. Fasten off with long tail.

You will need about fifty 10-inch pieces of tan yarn to finish the Snout. To quickly cut the strands, wrap yarn around a 5" x 5" piece of cardboard. On one side, insert scissors between cardboard and yarn—and cut. Sew a row of contrasting color basting sts down center of Snout (see turquoise line, Fig. A).

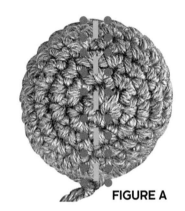

FIGURE A

Attach double strands of yarn through sts on each side of line (see red dots, Fig. A) using Fringe Technique (see page 16 and Fig. B). Remove basting sts.

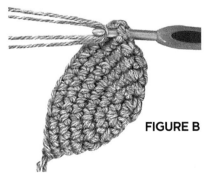

FIGURE B

ASSEMBLY

Sew Nose to Snout and use long tail of black yarn to embroider a 1/2-inch vertical st at base of Nose. Stuff Snout and gently squeeze into a horizontal oval shape. Sew Snout to Hat. Cut posts off animal eyes with wire cutters. Lay eyes in place to find position and mark with an outline of straight pins. At this point, I like to slip a piece of non-stick aluminum foil inside Hat in case any glue seeps thru a gap between sts. Hot glue eyes to Hat. Tie Ears to top of Hat. Trim Ear fringe even with lower edge of Ear Flaps. Trim Snout fringe even with lower edge of Hat. For eyebrows, thread yarn needle with a double-strand of yarn (1 tan and 1 brown) and embroider straight stitches over each eye (see Eyebrow Guide).

Eyebrow Guide

Note: If your Ears or Snout have wavy yarn and you'd prefer it to be straight as shown, you can straighten it out with a small garment steamer. Weave in ends. ◆

bald eagle

SIZES

Small [Medium; Large]

SUPPLIES

Worsted weight yarn in white 285 yds [365; 400]; dark brown 50 yds [65; 70]; yellow 25 yds; plus small amount of black

G6/4mm and J10/6mm [H8/5mm and J10/6mm; I9/5.5mm and J10/6mm] crochet hooks or size needed to obtain gauge

2 yellow animal eyes, 24mm

Needle and thread

Wire cutters

Stuffing

Stitch marker

Yarn needle

GAUGE

With J10/6mm hook and 2 strands of yarn held together:

5 rnds of sc = 3" diameter circle

HAT

The Hat is crocheted with alternating rounds of Single Crochet and Loop Stitch. Note: Loops will form on wrong side of work. Hat is turned loop-side out when done.

With J10/6mm hook and 2 strands of white yarn held together, make a magic ring, ch 1.

Rnd 1: 6 sc in ring, pull ring closed almost tight (6 sts).

Rnd 2: 2 lp st in each st around. Place marker for beginning of rnd and move marker up as each rnd is completed (12 sts).

Rnd 3: *sc in next st, 2 sc in next st* 6 times (18 sts).

Rnd 4: *lp st in next 2 sts, 2 lp st in next st* 6 times (24 sts).

Rnd 5: *sc in next 3 sts, 2 sc in next st* 6 times (30 sts).

Rnd 6: *lp st in next 4 sts, 2 lp st in next st* 6 times (36 sts).

Rnd 7: *sc in next 5 sts, 2 sc in next st* 6 times (42 sts).

Rnd 8: *lp st in next 6 sts, 2 lp st in next st* 6 times (48 sts).

Rnd 9: *sc in next 7 sts, 2 sc in next st* 6 times (54 sts).

Rnd 10: *lp st in next 8 sts, 2 lp st in next st* 6 times (60 sts).

• FOR SIZE SMALL:

Rnd 11: sc in each st around.

Rnd 12: lp st in each st around.

Rnds 13-25: continue alternating Rnds 11-12.

Fasten off.

• FOR SIZE MEDIUM:

Rnd 11: *sc in next 9 sts, 2 sc in next st* 6 times (66 sts).

Rnd 12: lp st in each st around.

Rnd 13: sc in each st around.

Rnd 14-27: continue alternating Rnds 12-13.

Fasten off.

• FOR SIZE LARGE:

Rnd 11: *sc in next 9 sts, 2 sc in next st* 6 times (66 sts).

Rnd 12: *lp st in next 10 sts, 2 lp st in next st* 6 times (72 sts).

Rnd 13: sc in each st around.

Rnd 14: lp st in each st around.

Rnd 15-29: continue alternating Rnds 13-14.

Fasten off.

EAR FLAP (MAKE 2)

Mark position of Ear Flaps (see page 14). Work Ear Flaps into sts between markers, not including marked sts.

• For size **Small,** work in the 10 sts between each set of markers.

• For size **Medium,** work in the 12 sts between each set of markers.

• For size **Large,** work in the 14 sts between each set of markers.

The Ear Flap is crocheted with alternating rows of Loop Stitch and Single Crochet. Note: A chain 1 at the beginning of a row is for turning your work and does not count as a stitch.

Row 1: With J10/6mm hook and 2 strands of brown yarn held together, fasten on in 1st st with lp st (see page 16, "Attaching with Single Crochet", but substitute lp st for sc), lp st in each remaining st across. Place marker for beginning of row and move marker up as each row is completed.

Row 2: ch 1, turn, skip next st, sc in each remaining st across.

Rows 3-end: Repeat Row 2, alternating rows of lp st and sc, until only 3 sc remain, ch 1, turn, insert hook in each st and pull up a loop. You will have 4 loops on hook. Yarn over and pull through all 4 loops. Fasten off. Weave in ends.

EDGE TRIM

Using J10/6mm hook and 2 strands of brown yarn held together, attach yarn at center back of Hat with sc. Sc in each st around perimeter of Hat making 3 sts in same st at tip of each Ear Flap. Fasten off.

BEAK

With G6/4mm [H8/5mm; I9/5.5mm] crochet hook and a single strand of yellow yarn, make a magic ring, ch 1.

Rnd 1: 6 sc in ring, pull ring closed tight (6 sts).

Rnds 2-3: sc in each st around. Place marker for beginning of rnd and move marker up as each rnd is completed.

Rnd 4: *sc in next st, 2 sc in next st* 3 times (9 sts).

Rnd 5: *sc in next 2 sts, 2 sc in next st* 3 times (12 sts).

Rnds 6-7: sc in each st around.

Rnd 8: *sc in next st, 2 sc in next st* 6 times (18 sts).

Rnds 9-10: sc in each st around.

Rnd 11: *sc in next 2 sts, 2 sc in next st* 6 times (24 sts).

Rnds 12-14: sc in each st around.

Rnd 15: *sc in next 3 sts, 2 sc in next st* 6 times (30 sts).

Rnds 16-18: sc in each st around.

Rnd 19: *sc in next 4 sts, 2 sc in next st* 6 times (36 sts).

Sl st in next st. Fasten off with long tail.

BEAKLINE

With J10/6mm hook and 2 strands of yellow yarn held together, ch 58 [60; 62]. Fasten off.

EYELID (MAKE 2)

With H8/5mm crochet hook and a single strand of white yarn, ch 2.

Note: A chain 1 at the beginning of a row is for turning your work and does not count as a stitch.

Row 1: 3 sc in 2nd ch from hook.

Row 2: ch 1, turn, 2 sc in next 3 sts (6 sts).

Row 3: ch 1, turn, *sc in next st, 2 sc in next st* 3 times (9 sts).

Continue across straight side making one sc in each st across. (Hold starting tail across straight side and crochet over tail as you work.) Sl st in next st. Fasten off with long tail.

EYE RIM (MAKE 2)

With H8/5mm crochet hook and a single strand of black yarn, make a magic ring, ch 1.

Rnd 1: 6 sc in ring, pull ring closed almost tight (6 sts).

Rnd 2: 2 sc in each st around (12 sts).

Sl st in next st. Fasten off with long tail.

ASSEMBLY

Cut loops of lp sts open. With soft brush, brush yarn backward—away from face. See photo for reference. Spray with water while brushing, if desired, to help train yarn into position. Flatten beak with long tail at center (see Fig. A).

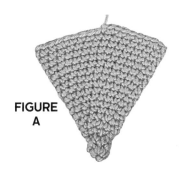

FIGURE A

Place center of Beakline 3 rnds below tip of Beak and arrange in a V-shape, parallel to Beak edge, as shown in Fig. B. Pin in place.

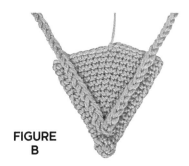

FIGURE B

Bring ends of Beakline to meet at tip of V (see Fig. C) and pin in place. Sew Beakline in position with needle and thread.

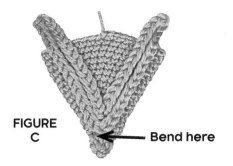

FIGURE C ← **Bend here**

Bend tip of Beak 90 degrees toward Beakline and tack in place. Stuff Beak. With black yarn, embroider 2 straight sts on top of Beak, about 1/2" long, for nostrils. Sew Beak to Hat. Attach animal eyes to center of Eye Rims. Clip off excess post with wire cutters. Sew Eyes to Hat. Sew Eyelids at an angle over Eyes. Trim straggly white yarn ends around bottom of Hat to meet brown edge. Trim around eyes if needed. Weave in ends. ♦

Add yellow tassels to Ear Flaps for a fun variation.

ladybug

SIZES

Small [Medium; Large]

SUPPLIES

Worsted weight yarn in red 230 yds [300; 320]; black 70 yds plus small amount of white

Size H8/5mm and J10/6mm crochet hooks or size needed to obtain gauge

2 white animal eyes, 15mm [18; 18]

Wire cutters

Stitch marker

Yarn needle

GAUGE

With J10/6mm hook and 2 strands of yarn held together:

5 rnds of sc = 3" diameter circle

HAT

With J10/6mm hook and 2 strands of red yarn held together, make a magic ring, ch 1.

Rnd 1: 6 sc in ring, pull ring closed tight (6 sts).

Rnd 2: 2 sc in each st around. Place marker for beginning of rnd and move marker up as each rnd is completed (12 sts).

Rnd 3: *sc in next st, 2 sc in next st* 6 times (18 sts).

Rnd 4: *sc in next 2 sts, 2 sc in next st* 6 times (24 sts).

Rnd 5: *sc in next 3 sts, 2 sc in next st* 6 times (30 sts).

Rnd 6: *sc in next 4 sts, 2 sc in next st* 6 times (36 sts).

Rnd 7: *sc in next 5 sts, 2 sc in next st* 6 times (42 sts).

Rnd 8: *sc in next 6 sts, 2 sc in next st* 6 times (48 sts).

Rnd 9: *sc in next 7 sts, 2 sc in next st* 6 times (54 sts).

Rnd 10: *sc in next 8 sts, 2 sc in next st* 6 times (60 sts).

• **FOR SIZE SMALL:**

Rnds 11-25: sc in each st around. Fasten off.

• **FOR SIZE MEDIUM:**

Rnd 11: *sc in next 9 sts, 2 sc in next st* 6 times (66 sts).

Rnds 12-27: sc in each st around. Fasten off.

• **FOR SIZE LARGE:**

Rnd 11: *sc in next 9 sts, 2 sc in next st* 6 times (66 sts).

Rnd 12: *sc in next 10 sts, 2 sc in next st* 6 times (72 sts).

Rnds 13-29: sc in each st around. Fasten off.

EAR FLAP (MAKE 2)

Mark position of Ear Flaps (see page 14). Work Ear Flaps into sts between markers, not including the marked sts.

• **For size Small,** work in the 10 sts between each set of markers.

• **For size Medium,** work in the 12 sts between each set of markers.

• **For size Large,** work in the 14 sts between each set of markers.

Note: A chain 1 at the beginning of a row is for turning your work and does not count as a stitch.

Row 1: With J10/6mm hook and 2 strands of red yarn held together, attach yarn in 1st st with sc, sc in each remaining st across. Place marker for beginning of row and move marker up as each row is completed.

Row 2: ch 1, turn, skip next st, sc in each remaining st across.

Rows 3-end: Repeat Row 2 until only 3 sc remain, ch 1, turn, insert hook in each st and pull up a loop. You will have 4 loops on hook. Yarn over and pull through all 4 loops.

Fasten off. Weave in ends.

EDGE TRIM

Using J10/6mm hook and 2 strands of black yarn held together, attach yarn at center back of Hat with sc. Sc in each st around perimeter of Hat making 3 sts in same st at tip of each Ear Flap. Fasten off.

TWISTED CORD TIE (MAKE 2)

Cut eight 54" strands of red yarn and eight 54" strands of black yarn. Follow instructions on page 15.

FACE

With H8/5mm hook and a single strand of black yarn, ch 2.

Note: A chain 1 at the beginning of a row is for turning your work and does not count as a stitch.

Row 1: 3 sc in 2nd ch from hook.

Row 2: ch 1, turn, 2 sc in next 3 sts (6 sts).

Row 3: ch 1, turn, *sc in next st, 2 sc in next st* 3 times (9 sts).

Row 4: ch 1, turn, *sc in next 2 sts, 2 sc in next st* 3 times (12 sts).

Row 5: ch 1, turn, *sc in next 3 sts, 2 sc in next st* 3 times (15 sts).

Row 6: ch 1, turn, *sc in next 4 sts, 2 sc in next st* 3 times (18 sts).

Row 7: ch 1, turn, *sc in next 5 sts, 2 sc in next st* 3 times (21 sts).

Row 8: ch 1, turn, *sc in next 6 sts, 2 sc in next st* 3 times (24 sts).

Row 9: ch 1, turn, *sc in next 7 sts, 2 sc in next st* 3 times (27 sts).

Stop here for Size Small and jump ahead to Edge Finish.

Row 10: ch 1, turn, *sc in next 8 sts, 2 sc in next st* 3 times (30 sts).

Row 11: ch 1, turn, *sc in next 9 sts, 2 sc in next st* 3 times (33 sts).

Stop here for Size Medium and jump ahead to Edge Finish.

Row 12: ch 1, turn, *sc in next 10 sts, 2 sc in next st* 3 times (36 sts).

Row 13: ch 1, turn, *sc in next 11 sts, 2 sc in next st* 3 times (39 sts).

Edge Finish: Continue working across straight side making one sc in each st across. Hold starting tail across straight side and crochet over tail as you work.

Sl st in next st. Fasten off with long tail.

ANTENNA (MAKE 2)

With J10/6mm hook and 2 strands of black yarn held together, ch 12 [13; 14] loosely. Sc in 2nd ch from hook. Fasten off with long tail.

DOTS (MAKE 14)

With H8/5mm hook and a single strand of black yarn, make a magic ring, ch 1.

Rnd 1: 6 sc in ring, pull ring closed tight (6 sts).

Rnd 2: 2 sc in each st around (12 sts).

Sl st in next st. Fasten off with long tail.

WINGS

Fold Hat in half so that Earflaps meet. Flatten and secure with pins. Using a single strand of black yarn, embroider along the crease with chain stitch embroidery (see page 17). Knot end to secure.

ASSEMBLY

Attach animal eyes to Face. Clip off excess post with wire cutters. Sew Face to Hat. Sew Antennae and Dots to Hat. With white yarn, embroider a V-shape for mouth. Weave in ends. ♦

snow leopard

SIZES

Small [Medium; Large]

SUPPLIES

Worsted weight yarn in light gray 425 yds [550; 610]; medium gray 85 yds and black 60 yds plus small amount of white

F5/3.75mm, G6/4mm, H8/5mm and J10/6mm [F5/3.75mm, H8/5mm and J10/6mm; F5/3.75mm, H8/5mm, I9/5.5mm, J10/6mm and K10.5/6.5mm] crochet hooks or size needed to obtain gauge

2 blue or green animal eyes, 24mm

Wire cutters

Sewing needle and thread

Stitch marker

Yarn needle

GAUGE

With J10/6mm hook and 2 strands of yarn held together:

5 rnds of sc = 3" diameter circle

HAT

With J10/6mm hook and 2 strands of light gray yarn held together, make a magic ring, ch 1.

Rnd 1: 6 sc in ring, pull ring closed tight (6 sts).

Rnd 2: 2 sc in each st around. Place marker for beginning of rnd and move marker up as each rnd is completed (12 sts).

Rnd 3: *sc in next st, 2 sc in next st* 6 times (18 sts).

Rnd 4: *sc in next 2 sts, 2 sc in next st* 6 times (24 sts).

Rnd 5: *sc in next 3 sts, 2 sc in next st* 6 times (30 sts).

Rnd 6: *sc in next 4 sts, 2 sc in next st* 6 times (36 sts).

Rnd 7: *sc in next 5 sts, 2 sc in next st* 6 times (42 sts).

Rnd 8: *sc in next 6 sts, 2 sc in next st* 6 times (48 sts).

Rnd 9: *sc in next 7 sts, 2 sc in next st* 6 times (54 sts).

Rnd 10: *sc in next 8 sts, 2 sc in next st* 6 times (60 sts).

• FOR SIZE SMALL:

Rnds 11-25: sc in each st around. Fasten off.

• FOR SIZE MEDIUM:

Rnd 11: *sc in next 9 sts, 2 sc in next st* 6 times (66 sts).

Rnds 12-27: sc in each st around. Fasten off.

• FOR SIZE LARGE:

Rnd 11: *sc in next 9 sts, 2 sc in next st* 6 times (66 sts).

Rnd 12: *sc in next 10 sts, 2 sc in next st* 6 times (72 sts).

Rnds 13-29: sc in each st around. Fasten off.

SCARF (MAKE 2)

Mark position of Scarf (see page 14). Work Scarf into sts between markers, not including marked sts.

• **For size Small,** work in the 10 sts between each set of markers.

• **For size Medium,** work in the 12 sts between each set of markers.

• **For size Large,** work in the 14 sts between each set of markers.

Note: A chain 1 at the beginning of a row is for turning your work and does not count as a stitch.

Row 1: With J10/6mm hook and 2 strands of light gray yarn held together, attach yarn in 1st st with sc, sc in each remaining st across. Place marker for beginning of row and move marker up as each row is completed.

Row 2: ch 1, turn, sc in each st across.

Rows 3-end: Repeat Row 2 until scarf is about 20" long.

EDGE TRIM

Using J10/6mm hook and 2 strands of light gray yarn held together, attach yarn at center back of Hat with sc. Sc in each st around perimeter of Hat and Scarves making 3 sts in same st at lower corners of Scarves. Fasten off.

NOSE

With G6/4mm [H8/5mm; I9/5.5mm] hook and a single strand of medium gray yarn, ch 9 loosely.

Note: A chain 1 at the beginning of a row is for turning your work and does not count as a stitch.

Row 1: sc in 2nd ch from hook and in each remaining ch across (8 sts).

Rows 2-10: ch 1, turn, sc in each st across; change to black yarn in last st (8 sts).

Row 11: ch 1, turn, sc2tog, sc in next 4 sts, sc2tog (6 sts).

Row 12: ch 1, turn, sc2tog, sc in next 2 sts, sc2tog (4 sts).

Row 13 ch 1, turn, sc2tog twice (2 sts).

Row 14: ch 1, turn, sc2tog (1 st).

Fasten off with long tail.

EYE RIM (MAKE 2)

With H8/5mm hook and a single strand of black yarn, make a magic ring, ch 1.

Rnd 1: 8 sc in ring, pull ring closed almost tight (8 sts).

Rnd 2a: 2 sc in next 3 sts (6 sts).

Point: ch 2 and sc in 2nd ch from hook, sc in next st.

Rnd 2b: 2 sc in next 3 sts (6 sts).

Point: ch 2 and sc in 2nd ch from hook, sc in next st.

Sl st in next st. Fasten off with long tail.

EAR (MAKE 2)

With H8/5mm [J10/6mm; K10.5/6.5mm] hook and 2 strands of light gray yarn held together, make a magic ring, ch 1.

Rnd 1: 6 sc in ring, pull ring closed tight (6 sts).

Rnd 2: 2 sc in each st around. Place marker for beginning of rnd and move marker up as each rnd is completed (12 sts).

Rnd 3: sc in each st around.

Rnd 4: *sc in next st, 2 sc in next st* 6 times (18 sts).

Rnd 5: *sc in next 2 sts, 2 sc in next st* 6 times (24 sts).

Rnd 6: *sc in next 3 sts, 2 sc in next st* 6 times (30 sts).

Rnds 7-11: sc in each st around.

Fasten off.

Flatten Ear. Sew layers together along open edge. Fold inner corner forward (see photo next page) and tack in place with a stitch.

SPOTS

The Snow Leopard's spots, which are also called "open rosettes", are made in 4 sizes and sewn to the Hat and Scarves with sewing thread. The Spots feature a simple "slip stitch-chain 1" outline which creates a cute jagged edge. The quantities indicated are approximate. Adjust as needed to get the look you like.

SMALL SPOT (MAKE APPROX. 21)

With F5/3.75mm hook and a single strand of medium gray yarn, make a magic ring, ch 1.

Rnd 1: 5 sc in ring, pull ring closed tight (5 sts).

Rnd 2: fasten on with black,*sl st, ch 1* in next 4 sts.

Sl st in next st. Fasten off. Weave in ends.

MEDIUM SPOT (MAKE APPROX. 16)

With F5/3.75mm hook and a single strand of medium gray yarn, make a magic ring, ch 1.

Rnd 1: 6 sc in ring, pull ring closed tight (6 sts).

Rnd 2: sc in 1st st, *hdc, dc* in next st, *dc, hdc* in next st, sl st in next st, *hdc, dc* in next st, *dc, sl st* in next st (10 sts).

Rnd 3: fasten on with black, *sl st, ch 1* in next 8 sts.

Sl st in next st. Fasten off. Weave in ends.

LARGE SPOT (MAKE APPROX. 12)

With F5/3.75mm hook and a single strand of medium gray yarn, make a magic ring, ch 1.

Rnd 1: 7 sc in ring, pull ring closed tight (7 sts).

Rnd 2: *sc, hdc* in 1st st, 2 dc in next st, *hdc, sc* in next st, *hdc, dc* in next st, 2 sc in next st, *hdc, dc* in next st, *hdc, sc* in next st (14 sts).

Rnd 3: fasten on with black, *sl st, ch 1* in next 12 sts.

Sl st in next st. Fasten off. Weave in ends.

EXTRA-LARGE SPOT (MAKE APPROX. 12)

With F5/3.75mm hook and a single strand of medium gray yarn, make a magic ring, ch 1.

Rnd 1: 8 sc in ring, pull ring closed tight (8 sts).

Rnd 2: 2 dc in 1st st, 2 hdc in next st, sl st in next st, *sl st, ch 2, dc* in next st, 3 dc in next st, 3 hdc in next st, *sl st, sc* in next st, sl st in next st (16 sts).

Rnd 3: fasten on with black, *sl st, ch 1* in next 14 sts.

Sl st in next st. Fasten off. Weave in ends.

ASSEMBLY

With a single strand of white yarn, embroider whiskers by making 1 stitch, about 2 1/2" long, for each whisker. Sew Nose to Hat. Insert animal eyes through center of Eye Rims and attach. Trim off excess post with wire cutters. Sew Eyes to Hat. Sew Ears slightly cupped to Hat. For toes, use black yarn to embroider 3 equidistant stitches on ends of Scarves. Pin Spots in place in an arrangement you like. (I like to use small and medium Spots on the head and a mixture of small, large and extra-large Spots on Scarves.) Sew Spots in place with sewing thread, sewing only through top loops of Scarves so stitches don't show on back side. Weave in ends. ♦

rabbit

SIZES

Small [Medium; Large]

SUPPLIES

Worsted weight yarn in tan 370 yds [475; 525] and white 50 yds plus small amount of pink

H8/5mm and J10/6mm [J10/6mm; J10/6mm and K10.5/6.5mm] crochet hooks or size needed to obtain gauge

2 black animal eyes, 24mm (or substitute black buttons)

Wire cutters

Hot glue gun (high temperature) and glue stick

Wire Brush

Stitch marker

Yarn needle

GAUGE

With J10/6mm hook and 2 strands of yarn held together:

5 rnds of sc = 3" diameter circle

HAT

With J10/6mm hook and 2 strands of tan yarn held together, make a magic ring, ch 1.

Rnd 1: 6 sc in ring, pull ring closed tight (6 sts).

Rnd 2: 2 sc in each st around. Place marker for beginning of rnd and move marker up as each rnd is completed (12 sts).

Rnd 3: *sc in next st, 2 sc in next st* 6 times (18 sts).

Rnd 4: *sc in next 2 sts, 2 sc in next st* 6 times (24 sts).

Rnd 5: *sc in next 3 sts, 2 sc in next st* 6 times (30 sts).

Rnd 6: *sc in next 4 sts, 2 sc in next st* 6 times (36 sts).

Rnd 7: *sc in next 5 sts, 2 sc in next st* 6 times (42 sts).

Rnd 8: *sc in next 6 sts, 2 sc in next st* 6 times (48 sts).

Rnd 9: *sc in next 7 sts, 2 sc in next st* 6 times (54 sts).

Rnd 10: *sc in next 8 sts, 2 sc in next st* 6 times (60 sts).

• FOR SIZE SMALL:

Rnds 11-25: sc in each st around. Fasten off.

• FOR SIZE MEDIUM:

Rnd 11: *sc in next 9 sts, 2 sc in next st* 6 times (66 sts).

Rnds 12-27: sc in each st around. Fasten off.

• FOR SIZE LARGE:

Rnd 11: *sc in next 9 sts, 2 sc in next st* 6 times (66 sts).

Rnd 12: *sc in next 10 sts, 2 sc in next st* 6 times (72 sts).

Rnds 13-29: sc in each st around. Fasten off.

EAR FLAP (MAKE 2)

Mark position of Ear Flaps (see page 14). Work Ear Flaps into sts between markers, not including the marked sts.

• **For size Small,** work in the 10 sts between each set of markers.

• **For size Medium,** work in the 12 sts between each set of markers.

• **For size Large,** work in the 14 sts between each set of markers.

Note: A chain 1 at the beginning of a row is for turning your work and does not count as a stitch.

Row 1: With J10/6mm hook and 2 strands of tan yarn held together, attach yarn in 1st st with sc, sc in each remaining st across. Place marker for beginning of row and move marker up as each row is completed.

Row 2: ch 1, turn, skip next st, sc in each remaining st across.

Rows 3-end: Repeat Row 2 until only 3 sc remain, ch 1, turn, insert

hook in each st and pull up a loop. You will have 4 loops on hook. Yarn over and pull through all 4 loops.

Fasten off. Weave in ends.

EDGE TRIM

Using J10/6mm hook and 2 strands of tan yarn held together, attach yarn at center back of Hat with sc. Sc in each st around perimeter of Hat making 3 sts in same st at tip of each Ear Flap. Fasten off.

EAR (MAKE 2)

With H8/5mm (J10/6mm: K10.5/6.5mm) hook and 2 strands of tan yarn held together, make a magic ring, ch 1.

Rnd 1: 6 sc in ring, pull ring closed tight (6 sts).

Rnd 2: *sc in next 2 sts, 2 sc in next st* 2 times. Place marker for beginning of rnd and move marker up as each rnd is completed (8 sts).

Rnd 3: *sc in next 3 sts, 2 sc in next st* 2 times (10 sts).

Rnd 4: *sc in next 4 sts, 2 sc in next st* 2 times (12 sts).

Rnd 5: *sc in next 5 sts, 2 sc in next st* 2 times (14 sts).

Rnd 6: *sc in next 6 sts, 2 sc in next st* 2 times (16 sts).

Rnd 7: *sc in next 7 sts, 2 sc in next st* 2 times (18 sts).

Rnd 8: *sc in next 8 sts, 2 sc in next st* 2 times (20 sts).

Rnd 9: *sc in next 9 sts, 2 sc in next st* 2 times (22 sts).

Rnd 10:: *sc in next 10 sts, 2 sc in next st* 2 times (24 sts).

Rnd 11-16: sc in each st around.

Rnd 17: sc in next 22 sts, sc2tog (23 sts).

Rnd 18: sc in each st around.

Rnd 19: sc in next 21 sts, sc2tog (22 sts).

Rnd 20: sc in each st around.

Rnd 21: sc in next 20 sts, sc2tog (21 sts).

Rnd 22: sc in each st around.

Rnd 23: sc in next 19 sts, sc2tog (20 sts).

Rnd 24: sc in each st around.

Rnd 25: sc in next 18 sts, sc2tog (19 sts).

Rnd 26: sc in each st around.

Rnd 27: sc in next 17 sts, sc2tog (18 sts).

Rnd 28: sc in each st around.

Rnd 29: sc in next 16 sts, sc2tog (17 sts).

Rnd 30: sc in each st around.

Rnd 31: sc in next 15 sts, sc2tog (16 sts).

Rnd 32: sc in each st around.

Rnd 33: sc in next 14 sts, sc2tog (15 sts).

Rnd 34: sc in each st around.

Rnd 35: sc in next 13 sts, sc2tog (14 sts).

Rnd 36: sc in each st around.

Rnd 37: sc in next 12 sts, sc2tog (13 sts).

Rnd 38: sc in each st around.

Rnd 39: sc in next 11 sts, sc2tog (12 sts).

Sl st in next st. Fasten off with long tail.

POM POM (MAKE 2)

Copy and cut out 2 Pom Pom Templates. Glue templates to lightweight cardboard. (A cereal box is a good weight.) Cut along black lines. Hold cardboard templates together so that notches align. Wrap white yarn evenly around ring, sliding yarn through notch and slit to begin each wrap. Wrap until inner circle is filled with yarn. Put 1 leg of scissors between cardboard rings and cut yarn apart around outer edge. Slide a double strand of tan yarn (about 18" long) between cardboard rings and tie ends together very tightly. Leave long tails for tying Pom Pom to Hat. Remove cardboard. Fluff yarn into a ball and trim surface into a nice, round shape.

ASSEMBLY

With a double strand of pink yarn, embroider a "Y" for the nose. Cut posts off animal eyes with wire cutters. Lay eyes in place to find position and mark with an outline of straight pins. At this point, I like to slip a piece of non-stick aluminum foil inside Hat in case any glue seeps thru a gap between sts. Hot glue eyes to Hat. Sew Ears to Hat. With wire brush (from hardware store or pet shop), brush Pom Poms until fibers separate and have a fuzzy appearance. Use tan tails to tie Pom Poms to Ear Flaps. Weave in ends. ♦

frog

SIZES

Small [Medium; Large]

SUPPLIES

Worsted weight yarn in green 245 yds [315; 350] and black 50 yds plus small amount of off-white (or white)

H8/5mm and J10/6mm [H8/5mm and J10/6mm; H8/5mm, J10/6mm and K10.5/6.5mm] crochet hooks or size needed to obtain gauge

2 black animal eyes, 18mm

Stuffing

Stitch marker

Yarn needle

GAUGE

With J10/6mm hook and 2 strands of yarn held together:

5 rnds of sc = 3" diameter circle

HAT

With J10/6mm hook and 2 strands of green yarn held together, make a magic ring, ch 1.

Rnd 1: 6 sc in ring, pull ring closed tight (6 sts).

Rnd 2: 2 sc in each st around. Place marker for beginning of rnd and move marker up as each rnd is completed (12 sts).

Rnd 3: *sc in next st, 2 sc in next st* 6 times (18 sts).

Rnd 4: *sc in next 2 sts, 2 sc in next st* 6 times (24 sts).

Rnd 5: *sc in next 3 sts, 2 sc in next st* 6 times (30 sts).

Rnd 6: *sc in next 4 sts, 2 sc in next st* 6 times (36 sts).

Rnd 7: *sc in next 5 sts, 2 sc in next st* 6 times (42 sts).

Rnd 8: *sc in next 6 sts, 2 sc in next st* 6 times (48 sts).

Rnd 9: *sc in next 7 sts, 2 sc in next st* 6 times (54 sts).

Rnd 10: *sc in next 8 sts, 2 sc in next st* 6 times (60 sts).

• FOR SIZE SMALL:

Rnds 11-23: sc in each st around; change to black yarn in last st.

Rnd 24: sc in each st around; change to green yarn in last st.

Rnd 25: sc in each st around. Fasten off.

• FOR SIZE MEDIUM:

Rnd 11: *sc in next 9 sts, 2 sc in next st* 6 times (66 sts).

Rnds 12-25: sc in each st around; change to black yarn in last st.

Rnd 26: sc in each st around; change to green yarn in last st.

Rnd 27: sc in each st around. Fasten off.

• FOR SIZE LARGE:

Rnd 11: *sc in next 9 sts, 2 sc in next st* 6 times (66 sts).

Rnd 12: *sc in next 10 sts, 2 sc in next st* 6 times (72 sts).

Rnds 13-27: sc in each st around; change to black yarn in last st.

Rnd 28: sc in each st around; change to green yarn in last st.

Rnd 29: sc in each st around. Fasten off.

EAR FLAP (MAKE 2)

Mark position of Ear Flaps (see page 14). Work Ear Flaps into sts between markers, not including the marked sts.

• **For size Small,** work in the 10 sts between each set of markers.

• **For size Medium,** work in the 12 sts between each set of markers.

• **For size Large,** work in the 14 sts between each set of markers.

Note: A chain 1 at the beginning of a row is for turning your work and does not count as a stitch.

Row 1: With J10/6mm hook and 2 strands of green yarn held together, attach yarn in 1st st with

sc, sc in each remaining st across. Place marker for beginning of row and move marker up as each row is completed.

Row 2: ch 1, turn, skip next st, sc in each remaining st across.

Rows 3-end: Repeat Row 2 until only 3 sc remain, ch 1, turn, insert hook in each st and pull up a loop. You will have 4 loops on hook. Yarn over and pull through all 4 loops.

Fasten off. Weave in ends.

EDGE TRIM

Using J10/6mm hook and 2 strands of black yarn held together, attach yarn at center back of Hat with sc. Sc in each st around perimeter of Hat making 3 sts in same st at tip of each Ear Flap. Fasten off.

TWISTED CORD TIE (MAKE 2)

Cut eight 54" strands of green yarn and eight 54" strands of black yarn. Follow instructions on page 15.

INNER EYE (MAKE 2)

With H8/5mm crochet hook and a single strand of off-white yarn, make a magic ring, ch 1.

Rnd 1: 6 sc in ring, pull ring closed almost tight (6 sts).

Rnd 2: 2 sc in each st around. Place marker for beginning of rnd and move marker up as each rnd is completed (12 sts).

Rnd 3: *sc in next st, 2 sc in next st* 6 times (18 sts).

Sl st in next st. Fasten off with long tail.

OUTER EYE (MAKE 2)

With H8/5mm [J10/6mm: K10.5/6.5mm] hook and 2 strands of green yarn held together, make a magic ring, ch 1.

Rnd 1: 6 sc in ring, pull ring closed tight (6 sts).

Rnd 2: 2 sc in each st around. Place marker for beginning of rnd and move marker up as each rnd is completed (12 sts).

Rnd 3: *sc in next st, 2 sc in next st* 6 times (18 sts).

Rnd 4: *sc in next 2 sts, 2 sc in next st* 6 times (24 sts).

Rnd 5: *sc in next 3 sts, 2 sc in next st* 6 times (30 sts).

Rnds 6-10: sc in each st around.

Fasten off with long tail.

ASSEMBLY

Insert posts of animal eyes through Inner Eyes, then through Outer Eyes and attach washer. Sew rim of Inner Eyes to Outer Eyes. Stuff Outer Eyes and sew to Hat. Note: I like to stuff lightly at first, then pack in more stuffing when I am almost done sewing to Hat. With a double strand of black yarn, embroider a small st for each nostril. Weave in ends. ♦

cat

SIZES

Small [Medium; Large]

SUPPLIES

Worsted weight yarn in medium gray 155 yds [200; 215], light gray 120 yds [150; 165] and pink 25 yds [30; 35] plus small amount of black and white

Size G6/4mm, H8/5mm and J10/6mm [G6/4mm, H8/5mm and J10/6mm; G6/4mm, H8/5mm, J10/6mm and K10.5/6.5mm] crochet hooks or size needed to obtain gauge

2 green cat eyes, 24mm

Wire cutters

Stitch marker

Yarn needle

GAUGE

With J10/6mm hook and 2 strands of yarn held together:

5 rnds of sc = 3" diameter circle

HAT

The Hat is made by alternating 2 rnds of light gray with 2 rnds of medium gray. Change to alternate color in last st of every other rnd.

With J10/6mm hook and 2 strands of light gray yarn held together, make a magic ring, ch 1.

Rnd 1: 6 sc in ring, pull ring closed tight (6 sts).

Rnd 2: 2 sc in each st around. Place marker for beginning of rnd and move marker up as each rnd is completed (12 sts).

Rnd 3: *sc in next st, 2 sc in next st* 6 times (18 sts).

Rnd 4: *sc in next 2 sts, 2 sc in next st* 6 times (24 sts).

Rnd 5: *sc in next 3 sts, 2 sc in next st* 6 times (30 sts).

Rnd 6: *sc in next 4 sts, 2 sc in next st* 6 times (36 sts).

Rnd 7: *sc in next 5 sts, 2 sc in next st* 6 times (42 sts).

Rnd 8: *sc in next 6 sts, 2 sc in next st* 6 times (48 sts).

Rnd 9: *sc in next 7 sts, 2 sc in next st* 6 times (54 sts).

Rnd 10: *sc in next 8 sts, 2 sc in next st* 6 times (60 sts).

• FOR SIZE SMALL:

Rnds 11-25: sc in each st around. You will end with 1 rnd of medium gray. Fasten off.

• FOR SIZE MEDIUM:

Rnd 11: *sc in next 9 sts, 2 sc in next st* 6 times (66 sts).

Rnds 12-27: sc in each st around. You will end with 1 rnd of medium gray. Fasten off.

• FOR SIZE LARGE:

Rnd 11: *sc in next 9 sts, 2 sc in next st* 6 times (66 sts).

Rnd 12: *sc in next 10 sts, 2 sc in next st* 6 times (72 sts).

Rnds 13-29: sc in each st around. You will end with 1 rnd of medium gray. Fasten off.

EAR FLAP (MAKE 2)

Mark position of Ear Flaps (see page 14). Work Ear Flaps into sts between markers, not including the marked sts.

• **For size Small,** work in the 10 sts between each set of markers.

• **For size Medium,** work in the 12 sts between each set of markers.

• **For size Large,** work in the 14 sts between each set of markers.

Note: A chain 1 at the beginning of a row is for turning your work and does not count as a stitch.

Row 1: With J10/6mm hook and 2 strands of medium gray yarn held together, attach yarn in 1st st with sc, sc in each remaining st across; change to light gray yarn in last st. Place marker for beginning of row and move marker up as each row is completed.

The rest of the Ear Flap is made by alternating 2 rnds of light gray with 2 rnds of medium gray. Change to alternate color in last st of every other rnd.

Row 2: ch 1, turn, skip next st, sc in each remaining st across.

Rows 3-end: Repeat Row 2 until only 3 sc remain, ch 1, turn, insert hook in each st and pull up a loop. You will have 4 loops on hook. Yarn over and pull through all 4 loops.

Fasten off. Weave in ends.

EDGE TRIM

Using J10/6mm hook and 2 strands of medium gray yarn held together, attach yarn at center back of Hat with sc. Sc in each st around perimeter of Hat making 3 sts in same st at tip of each Ear Flap. Fasten off.

TWISTED CORD TIE (MAKE 2)

Cut eight 54" strands of medium gray yarn and eight 54" strands of light gray yarn. Follow instructions on page 15.

EAR (MAKE 2)

With hook size H8/5mm [J10/6mm; K10.5/6.5mm] and 2 strands of pink yarn held together, chain 2 loosely.

Note: A chain 1 at the beginning of a row is for turning your work and does not count as a stitch.

Row 1: 3 sc in 2nd chain from hook (3 sts).

Row 2: ch 1, turn, 2 sc in next st, sc in next 2 sts (4 sts).

Row 3: ch 1, turn, 2 sc in next st, sc in next 3 sts (5 sts).

Row 4: ch 1, turn, 2 sc in next st, sc in next 4 sts (6 sts).

Row 5: ch 1, turn, 2 sc in next st, sc in next 5 sts (7 sts).

Row 6: ch 1, turn, 2 sc in next st, sc in next 6 sts (8 sts).

Row 7: ch 1, turn, 2 sc in next st, sc in next 7 sts (9 sts).

Row 8: ch 1, turn, 2 sc in next st, sc in next 8 sts (10 sts).

Row 9: ch 1, turn, 2 sc in next st, sc in next 9 sts (11 sts).

Fasten off.

Repeat with medium gray yarn, but do not fasten off. Place pink piece against gray piece wrong sides together, tucking loose ends between layers.

Rnd 1: sc around perimeter working each st through both ear pieces and making 3 sts at each corner.

Rnd 2: ch 1, turn, sc in each st around top 2 sides of Ear (not bottom edge).

Fasten off with long tail. Push sts from Rnd 2 inward toward pink layer to make a neat edge.

NOSE

With G6/4mm hook and a single strand of pink yarn, chain 2.

Note: A chain 1 at the beginning of a row is for turning your work and does not count as a stitch.

Row 1: 3 sc in 2nd chain from hook (3 sts).

Row 2: ch 1, turn, 2 sc in next st, sc in next 2 sts (4 sts).

Row 3: ch 1, turn, 2 sc in next st, sc in next 3 sts (5 sts).

Rnd 4: do not turn. Continue working forward and sl st in each st along next 2 sides making 3 sts in same st at corners.

Fasten off with long tail. Pinch tips into nice points.

EYE RIM (MAKE 2)

With H8/5mm hook and a single strand of black yarn, make a magic ring, ch 1.

Rnd 1: 8 sc in ring, pull ring closed almost tight (8 sts).

Rnd 2a: 2 sc in next 3 sts (6 sts).

Point: ch 2 and sc in 2nd ch from hook, sc in next st.

Rnd 2b: 2 sc in next 3 sts (6 sts).

Point: ch 2 and sc in 2nd ch from hook, sc in next st.

Sl st in next st. Fasten off with long tail.

ASSEMBLY

Sew Ears slightly cupped to top of Hat. With a single strand of white yarn, embroider whiskers by making 1 stitch, about 2 1/2" long, for each whisker. Sew Nose to Hat. Attach animal eyes to center of Eye Rims so that rims will be angled and pupils vertical when sewn to Hat. Clip off excess post with wire cutters. Sew Eyes to Hat. Weave in ends. ♦

mallard

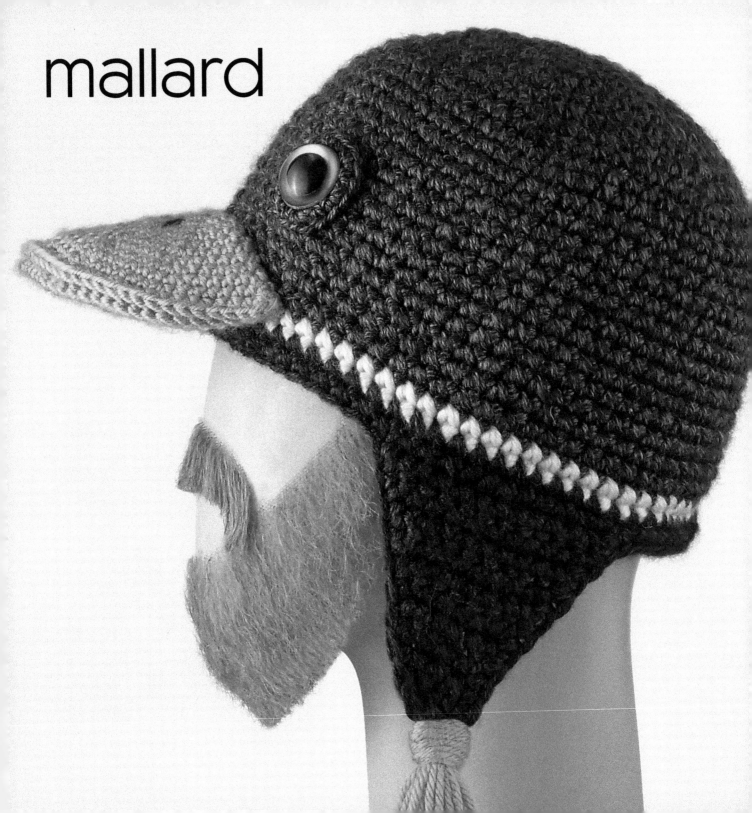

SIZES

Small [Medium; Large]

SUPPLIES

Worsted weight yarn in dark green 180 yds [230; 255]; yellow 50 yds; brown 40 yds; orange 20 yds; plus small amount of white and black

G6/4mm, H8/5mm and J10/6mm [H8/5mm and J10/6mm; H8/5mm, I9/5.5mm and J10/6mm] crochet hooks or size needed to obtain gauge

2 copper or yellow animal eyes, 24mm

Sewing needle and thread

1 sheet yellow craft foam, 9"x12"

Wire cutters

Stitch marker

Yarn needle

GAUGE

With J10/6mm hook and 2 strands of yarn held together:

5 rnds of sc = 3" diameter circle

HAT

With J10/6mm hook and 2 strands of dark green yarn held together, make a magic ring, ch 1.

Rnd 1: 6 sc in ring, pull ring closed tight (6 sts).

Rnd 2: 2 sc in each st around. Place marker for beginning of rnd and move marker up as each rnd is completed (12 sts).

Rnd 3: *sc in next st, 2 sc in next st* 6 times (18 sts).

Rnd 4: *sc in next 2 sts, 2 sc in next st* 6 times (24 sts).

Rnd 5: *sc in next 3 sts, 2 sc in next st* 6 times (30 sts).

Rnd 6: *sc in next 4 sts, 2 sc in next st* 6 times (36 sts).

Rnd 7: *sc in next 5 sts, 2 sc in next st* 6 times (42 sts).

Rnd 8: *sc in next 6 sts, 2 sc in next st* 6 times (48 sts).

Rnd 9: *sc in next 7 sts, 2 sc in next st* 6 times (54 sts).

Rnd 10: *sc in next 8 sts, 2 sc in next st* 6 times (60 sts).

• FOR SIZE SMALL:

Rnds 11-23: sc in each st around; change to white yarn in last st.

Rnd 24: sc in each st around; change to brown yarn in last st.

Rnd 25: sc in each st around.

Fasten off.

• FOR SIZE MEDIUM:

Rnd 11: *sc in next 9 sts, 2 sc in next st* 6 times (66 sts).

Rnds 12-25: sc in each st around; change to white yarn in last st.

Rnd 26: sc in each st around; change to brown yarn in last st.

Rnd 27: sc in each st around.

Fasten off.

• FOR SIZE LARGE:

Rnd 11: *sc in next 9 sts, 2 sc in next st* 6 times (66 sts).

Rnd 12: *sc in next 10 sts, 2 sc in next st* 6 times (72 sts).

Rnds 13-27: sc in each st around; change to white yarn in last st.

Rnd 28: sc in each st around; change to brown yarn in last st.

Rnd 29: sc in each st around.

Fasten off.

EAR FLAP (MAKE 2)

Mark position of Ear Flaps (see page 14). Work Ear Flaps into sts between markers, not including the marked sts.

• **For size Small,** work in the 10 sts between each set of markers.

• **For size Medium,** work in the 12 sts between each set of markers.

• **For size Large,** work in the 14 sts between each set of markers.

Note: A chain 1 at the beginning of a row is for turning your work and does not count as a stitch.

Row 1: With J10/6mm hook and 2 strands of brown yarn held together, attach yarn in 1st st with sc, sc in each remaining st across. Place marker for beginning of row and move marker up as each row is completed.

Row 2: ch 1, turn, skip next st, sc in each remaining st across.

Rows 3-end: Repeat Row 2 until only 3 sc remain, ch 1, turn, insert hook in each st and pull up a loop. You will have 4 loops on hook. Yarn over and pull through all 4 loops.

Fasten off. Weave in ends.

EDGE TRIM

Using J10/6mm hook and 2 strands of brown yarn held together, attach yarn at center back of Hat with sc. Sc in each st around perimeter of Hat making 3 sts in same st at tip of each Ear Flap. Fasten off.

TASSEL (MAKE 2)

Cut sixteen 20-inch pieces of orange yarn. Insert a large hook through tip of Ear Flap from back to front and follow instructions for Fringe Technique, page 16.

Note: You won't be able to fit all pieces of yarn on hook at one time. Pull strands through in 2 or 3 groups. Once your knot has been made, pull on each strand to tighten. Trim to 5".

EYE RIM (MAKE 2)

With H8/5mm hook and a single strand of dark green yarn, make a magic ring, ch 1.

Rnd 1: 6 sc in ring, pull ring closed almost tight (6 sts).

Rnd 2: 2 sc in each st around. Place marker for beginning of rnd and move marker up as each rnd is completed (12 sts).

Rnd 3: *sc in next st, 2 sc in next st* 6 times (18 sts).

Fasten off with long tail.

BILL

With G6/4mm [H8/5mm; I9/5.5mm] hook and a single strand of yellow yarn, make a magic ring, ch 1.

Rnd 1: 6 sc in ring, pull ring closed tight (6 sts).

Rnd 2: 2 sc in each st around. Place marker for beginning of rnd and move marker up as each rnd is completed (12 sts).

Rnd 3: 2 sc in each st around (24 sts).

Rnd 4: *sc in next st, 2 sc in next st* 12 times (36 sts).

Rnd 5: *sc in next 2 sts, 2 sc in next st* 12 times (48 sts).

Rnd 6: sc in each st around.

Rnd 7: *sc in next 3 sts, 2 sc in next st* 12 times (60 sts).

Rnd 8: sc in each st around.

Rnd 9: *sc in next 4 sts, 2 sc in next st* 12 times (72 sts).

Rnd 10: sc in each st around.

Rnd 11: *sc in next 5 sts, 2 sc in next st* 12 times (84 sts).

Rnd 12: sc in each st around.

Rnd 13: *sc in next 6 sts, 2 sc in next st* 12 times (96 sts).

Rnd 14: sc in each st around.

Sl st in next st. Fasten off. Fold Bill in half wrong sides together.

Place folded Bill on craft foam and trace an outline. Cut it out about 1/2" smaller than outline on all sides. Insert foam between layers of Bill. With sewing needle and thread, stitch layers of Bill together, stitching in the groove between Rnds 13 and 14 (see arrow on photo below).

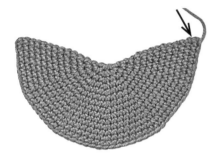

ASSEMBLY

Using sewing needle and thread, sew Bill to Hat, slightly arched, with ends meeting white stripe. For nostrils, use a double strand of black yarn to embroider two straight stitches: Insert needle under top layer of Bill from inside Hat and work through top layer only so sts don't show on underside of Bill. Attach animal eyes to center of Eye Rims. Clip off excess post with wire cutters. Sew Eyes to Hat. Weave in ends. ♦

sheep

SIZES

Small [Medium; Large]

SUPPLIES

Worsted weight yarn in off-white 385 yds [480; 525] and pink 25 yds [30; 35] plus small amount of black

H8/5mm and J10/6mm [J10/6mm; J10/6mm and K10.5/6.5mm] crochet hooks or size needed to obtain gauge

2 brown animal eyes, 24mm (or substitute black buttons)

Wire cutters

Hot glue gun (high temperature) and glue stick

Stitch marker

Yarn needle

GAUGE

With J10/6mm hook and 2 strands of yarn held together:

5 rnds of sc = 3" diameter circle

HAT

The Hat is crocheted with alternating rounds of Single Crochet and Loop Stitch. Note: Loops will form on wrong side of work. Hat is turned loop-side out when done.

With J10/6mm hook and 2 strands of off-white yarn held together, make a magic ring, ch 1.

Rnd 1: 6 sc in ring, pull ring closed loosely (6 sts).

Rnd 2: 2 lp st in each st around. Place marker for beginning of rnd and move marker up as each rnd is completed (12 sts).

Rnd 3: *sc in next st, 2 sc in next st* 6 times (18 sts).

Rnd 4: *lp st in next 2 sts, 2 lp st in next st* 6 times (24 sts).

Rnd 5: *sc in next 3 sts, 2 sc in next st* 6 times (30 sts).

Rnd 6: *lp st in next 4 sts, 2 lp st in next st* 6 times (36 sts).

Rnd 7: *sc in next 5 sts, 2 sc in next st* 6 times (42 sts).

Rnd 8: *lp st in next 6 sts, 2 lp st in next st* 6 times (48 sts).

Rnd 9: *sc in next 7 sts, 2 sc in next st* 6 times (54 sts).

Rnd 10: *lp st in next 8 sts, 2 lp st in next st* 6 times (60 sts).

• FOR SIZE SMALL:

Rnd 11: sc in each st around.

Rnd 12: lp st in each st around.

Rnd 13: sc in each st around.

Rnd 14: *lp st in next 6 sts, sc in next 12 sts, lp st in next 42 sts* (60 sts).

Rnd 15: sc in each st around.

Rnd 16: *lp st in next 5 sts, sc in next 14 sts, lp st in next 41 sts* (60 sts).

Rnd 17: sc in each st around.

Rnd 18: *lp st in next 4 sts, sc in next 16 sts, lp st in next 40 sts* (60 sts).

Rnd 19: sc in each st around.

Rnd 20: *lp st in next 3 sts, sc in next 18 sts, lp st in next 39 sts* (60 sts).

Rnd 21: sc in each st around.

Rnd 22: *lp st in next 2 sts, sc in next 20 sts, lp st in next 38 sts* (60 sts).

Rnd 23: sc in each st around.

Rnd 24: *lp st in next st, sc in next 22 sts, lp st in next 37 sts* (60 sts).

Rnd 25: sc in each st around.

Fasten off.

• FOR SIZE MEDIUM:

Rnd 11: *sc in next 9 sts, 2 sc in next st* 6 times (66 sts).

Rnd 12: lp st in each st around (66 sts).

Rnd 13: sc in each st around.

Rnd 14: lp st in each st around.

Rnd 15: sc in each st around.

Rnd 16: *lp st in next 6 sts, sc in

next 14 sts, lp st in next 46 sts* (66 sts).

Rnd 17: sc in each st around.

Rnd 18: *lp st in next 5 sts, sc in next 16 sts, lp st in next 45 sts* (66 sts).

Rnd 19: sc in each st around.

Rnd 20: *lp st in next 4 sts, sc in next 18 sts, lp st in next 44 sts* (66 sts).

Rnd 21: sc in each st around.

Rnd 22: *lp st in next 3 sts, sc in next 20 sts, lp st in next 43 sts* (66 sts).

Rnd 23: sc in each st around.

Rnd 24: *lp st in next 2 sts, sc in next 22 sts, lp st in next 42 sts* (66 sts)..

Rnd 25: sc in each st around.

Rnd 26: *lp st in next st, sc in next 24 sts, lp st in next 41 sts* (66 sts).

Rnd 27: sc in each st around.

Fasten off.

• **FOR SIZE LARGE:**

Rnd 11: *sc in next 9 sts, 2 sc in next st* 6 times (66 sts).

Rnd 12: *lp st in next 10 sts, 2 lp st in next st* 6 times (72 sts).

Rnd 13: sc in each st around.

Rnd 14: lp st in each st around.

Rnd 15: sc in each st around.

Rnd 16: lp st in each st around.

Rnd 17: sc in each st around.

Rnd 18: *lp st in next 6 sts, sc in next 16 sts, lp st in next 50 sts* (72 sts).

Rnd 19: sc in each st around.

Rnd 20: *lp st in next 5 sts, sc in next 18 sts, lp st in next 49 sts* (72 sts).

Rnd 21: sc in each st around.

Rnd 22: *lp st in next 4 sts, sc in next 20 sts, lp st in next 48 sts* (72 sts).

Rnd 23: sc in each st around.

Rnd 24: *lp st in next 3 sts, sc in next 22 sts, lp st in next 47 sts* (72 sts).

Rnd 25: sc in each st around.

Rnd 26: *lp st in next 2 sts, sc in next 24 sts, lp st in next 46 sts* (72 sts).

Rnd 27: sc in each st around.

Rnd 28: *lp st in next st, sc in next 26 sts, lp st in next 45 sts* (72 sts).

Rnd 29: sc in each st around.

Fasten off.

EAR FLAP (MAKE 2)

Use stitch markers to mark placement of Ear Flaps. They are worked in the 10 [12; 14] sts on each side of face.

Note: A chain 1 at the beginning of a row is for turning your work and does not count as a stitch.

Use J10/6mm hook and 2 strands of off-white yarn held together.

Row 1: fasten on and lp st in next 10 [12; 14] sts. Place marker for beginning of row and move marker up as each row is completed.

Row 2: ch 1, turn, skip next st, sc in each remaining st across.

Rows 3-end: repeat Row 2, alternating rows of lp st with rows of sc, until only 3 sts remain; then ch 1, turn, insert hook in each st and pull up a loop. You will have 4 loops on hook. Yarn over and pull through all 4 loops.

Fasten off. Weave in ends.

EDGE TRIM

Turn Hat loop-side out. Using J10/6mm hook and 2 strands of off-white yarn held together, attach yarn at center back of Hat with sc. Sc in each st around perimeter of Hat making 3 sts in same st at tip of each Ear Flap. Fasten off.

TWISTED CORD TIE (MAKE 2)

Cut sixteen 54" strands of off-white yarn. Follow instructions on page 15.

EAR (MAKE 2)

With hook size H8/5mm [J10/6mm; K10.5/6.5mm] and 2 strands of pink yarn held together, chain 2 loosely.

Note: A chain 1 at the beginning of a row is for turning your work and does not count as a stitch.

Row 1: 3 sc in 2nd chain from hook (3 sts).

Row 2: ch 1, turn, 2 sc in next st, sc in next st, 2 sc in next st (5 sts).

Row 3: ch 1, turn, 2 sc in next st, sc in next 3 sts, 2 sc in next st (7 sts).

Row 4: ch 1, turn, 2 sc in next st, sc in next 5 sts, 2 sc in next st (9 sts).

Row 5: ch 1, turn, 2 sc in next st, sc in next 7 sts, 2 sc in next st (11 sts).

Row 6: ch 1, turn, 2 sc in next st, sc in next 9 sts, 2 sc in next st (13 sts).

Rows 7-11: ch 1, turn, sc in each st across (13 sts).

Fasten off.

Repeat with off-white yarn, but do not fasten off. Place pink piece against off-white piece wrong sides together, tucking loose ends between layers.

Rnd 1: sc around perimeter working each st through both ear pieces and making 3 sts at each corner.

Rnd 2: sc in each st around next 2 sides.

Fasten off with long tail. Push sts from Rnd 2 inward toward pink layer to make a neat edge. Pull 1 strand of tail through opposite corner and tie both strands together so that lower tips of Ear meet. This will form a circular shape at base of Ear. Knot securely.

ASSEMBLY

With a double strand of black yarn, embroider a "T" for the nose. Cut posts off animal eyes with wire cutters. Lay eyes in place to find position and mark with an outline of straight pins. At this point, I like to slip a piece of non-stick aluminum foil inside Hat in case any glue seeps thru a gap between sts. Hot glue eyes to Hat. Locate placement for Ears and push loops of Hat out of the way. Sew Ears securely to Hat. Weave in ends. ♦

bee

SIZES

Small [Medium; Large]

SUPPLIES

Worsted weight yarn in yellow 100 yds [120; 135]; black 80 yds [100; 110]; and off-white 50 yds

H8/5mm and J10/6mm [H8/5mm and J10/6mm; H8/5mm, J10/6mm and K10.5/6.5mm] crochet hooks or size needed to obtain gauge

2 white animal eyes, 15mm

Sewing needle and thread

Stuffing

Stitch marker

Yarn needle

GAUGE

With J10/6mm hook and 2 strands of yarn held together:

5 rnds of sc = 3" diameter circle

HAT

With J10/6mm hook and 2 strands of yellow yarn held together, make a magic ring, ch 1.

Rnd 1: 6 sc in ring, pull ring closed tight (6 sts).

Rnd 2: 2 sc in each st around. Place marker for beginning of rnd and move marker up as each rnd is completed (12 sts).

Rnd 3: *sc in next st, 2 sc in next st* 6 times (18 sts).

Rnd 4: *sc in next 2 sts, 2 sc in next st* 6 times (24 sts).

Rnd 5: *sc in next 3 sts, 2 sc in next st* 6 times (30 sts).

Rnd 6: *sc in next 4 sts, 2 sc in next st* 6 times (36 sts).

Rnd 7: *sc in next 5 sts, 2 sc in next st* 6 times (42 sts).

Rnd 8: *sc in next 6 sts, 2 sc in next st* 6 times (48 sts).

• FOR SIZE SMALL

Rnd 9: *sc in next 7 sts, 2 sc in next st* 6 times; change to black yarn in last st (54 sts).

Rnd 10: *sc in next 8 sts, 2 sc in next st* 6 times (60 sts).

Rnd 11: sc in each st around; change to yellow yarn in last st.

Rnds 12-25: sc in each st around alternating 2 rnds of yellow with 2 rnds of black; change to alternate color in last st of every other rnd. Fasten off.

• FOR SIZE MEDIUM:

Rnd 9: *sc in next 7 sts, 2 sc in next st* 6 times (54 sts).

Rnd 10: *sc in next 8 sts, 2 sc in next st* 6 times (60 sts).

Rnd 11: *sc in next 9 sts, 2 sc in next st* 6 times; change to black yarn in last st (66 sts).

Rnds 12-27: sc in each st around alternating 2 rnds of black with 2 rnds of yellow; change to alternate color in last st of every other rnd. Fasten off.

• FOR SIZE LARGE:

Rnd 9: *sc in next 7 sts, 2 sc in next st* 6 times; change to black yarn in last st (54 sts).

Rnd 10: *sc in next 8 sts, 2 sc in next st* 6 times (60 sts).

Rnd 11: *sc in next 9 sts, 2 sc in next st* 6 times; change to yellow yarn in last st (66 sts).

Rnd 12: *sc in next 10 sts, 2 sc in next st* 6 times (72 sts).

Rnd 13: sc in each st around; change to black yarn in last st.

Rnds 14-29: sc in each st around alternating 2 rnds of black with 2 rnds of yellow; change to alternate color in last st of every other rnd. Fasten off.

EAR FLAP (MAKE 2)

Mark position of Ear Flaps (see page 14). Work Ear Flaps into sts between markers, not including the marked sts.

• **For size Small,** work in the 10 sts between each set of markers.

• **For size Medium,** work in the 12 sts between each set of markers.

• **For size Large,** work in the 14 sts between each set of markers.

Note: A chain 1 at the beginning of a row is for turning your work and does not count as a stitch.

Row 1: With J10/6mm hook and 2 strands of off-white yarn held together, attach yarn in 1st st with sc, sc in each remaining st across. Place marker for beginning of row and move marker up as each row is completed.

Row 2: ch 1, turn, skip next st, sc in each remaining st across.

Rows 3-end: Repeat Row 2 until only 3 sc remain, ch 1, turn, insert hook in each st and pull up a loop. You will have 4 loops on hook. Yarn over and pull through all 4 loops.

Fasten off. Weave in ends.

EDGE TRIM

Using J10/6mm hook and 2 strands of black yarn held together, attach yarn at back of Hat with sc. Sc in each st around perimeter of Hat changing to off-white yarn around Ear Flaps and making 3 sts in same st at tip of each Ear Flap. Fasten off.

HEAD

With hook size H8/5mm [J10/6mm; K10.5/6.5mm] and 2 strands of black yarn held together, make a magic ring, ch 1.

Rnd 1: 6 sc in ring, pull ring closed tight (6 sts).

Rnd 2: 2 sc in each st around. Place marker for beginning of rnd and move marker up as each rnd is completed (12 sts).

Rnd 3: *sc in next st, 2 sc in next st* 6 times (18 sts).

Rnd 4: *sc in next 2 sts, 2 sc in next st* 6 times (24 sts).

Rnds 5-7: sc in each st around.

Sl st in next st. Fasten off with long tail.

ANTENNA (MAKE 2)

With H8/5mm hook and 2 strands of black yarn held together, ch 10 tightly. Fasten off. Cut yarn close to knot at one end.

ASSEMBLY

Attach animal eyes to Head. With sewing needle and thread, sew Antennae to Head. Run needle up and down through center of Antennae for extra stiffening. Stuff Head and sew to Hat. Weave in ends. ♦

bear

SIZES

Small [Medium; Large]

SUPPLIES

Worsted weight yarn in brown 400
 yds [525; 585]; and tan 50 yds
 plus small amount of black

F5/3.75mm, G6/4mm, H8/5mm
 and J10/6mm [G6/4mm,
 H8/5mm and J10/6mm;
 H8/5mm, I9/5.5mm, J10/6mm,
 and K10.5/6.5mm] crochet
 hooks or size needed to
 obtain gauge

2 brown animal eyes, 24mm

Wire cutters

Sewing needle and thread

Stitch marker

Yarn needle

GAUGE

With J10/6mm hook and 2 strands
 of yarn held together:

5 rnds of sc = 3" diameter circle

HAT

With J10/6mm hook and 2 strands
 of brown yarn held together,
 make a magic ring, ch 1.

Rnd 1: 6 sc in ring, pull ring closed
 tight (6 sts).

Rnd 2: 2 sc in each st around.
Place marker for beginning of rnd
and move marker up as each rnd
is completed (12 sts).

Rnd 3: *sc in next st, 2 sc in next
st* 6 times (18 sts).

Rnd 4: *sc in next 2 sts, 2 sc in
next st* 6 times (24 sts).

Rnd 5: *sc in next 3 sts, 2 sc in
next st* 6 times (30 sts).

Rnd 6: *sc in next 4 sts, 2 sc in
next st* 6 times (36 sts).

Rnd 7: *sc in next 5 sts, 2 sc in next
st* 6 times (42 sts).

Rnd 8: *sc in next 6 sts, 2 sc in
next st* 6 times (48 sts).

Rnd 9: *sc in next 7 sts, 2 sc in
next st* 6 times (54 sts).

Rnd 10: *sc in next 8 sts, 2 sc in
next st* 6 times (60 sts).

• FOR SIZE SMALL:

Rnds 11-25: sc in each st around.
Fasten off.

• FOR SIZE MEDIUM:

Rnd 11: *sc in next 9 sts, 2 sc in
next st* 6 times (66 sts).

Rnds 12-27: sc in each st around.
Fasten off.

• FOR SIZE LARGE:

Rnd 11: *sc in next 9 sts, 2 sc in
next st* 6 times (66 sts).

Rnd 12: *sc in next 10 sts, 2 sc in
next st* 6 times (72 sts).

Rnds 13-29: sc in each st around.
Fasten off.

SCARF (MAKE 2)

Mark position of Scarf (see page
14). Work Scarf into sts between
markers, not including marked sts.

• **For size Small,** work in the 10 sts
between each set of markers.

• **For size Medium,** work in the 12
sts between each set of markers.

• **For size Large,** work in the 14
sts between each set of markers.

Note: A chain 1 at the beginning of
a row is for turning your work and
does not count as a stitch.

Row 1: With J10/6mm hook and
2 strands of brown yarn held
together, attach yarn in 1st st with
sc, sc in each remaining st across.
Place marker for beginning of row
and move marker up as each
row is completed.

Row 2: ch 1, turn, sc in each st
across.

Rows 3-end: Repeat Row 2 until
scarf is about 20" long.

EDGE TRIM

Using J10/6mm hook and 2 strands of tan yarn held together, attach yarn at center back of Hat with sc. Sc in each st around perimeter of Hat and Scarves making 3 sts in same st at lower corners of Scarves. Fasten off.

OUTER EAR (MAKE 2)

With hook size H8/5mm [J10/6mm; K10.5/6.5mm] and 2 strands of brown yarn held together, make a magic ring, ch 1.

Rnd 1: 6 sc in ring, pull ring closed tight (6 sts).

Rnd 2: 2 sc in each st around. Place marker for beginning of rnd and move marker up as each rnd is completed (12 sts).

Rnd 3: *sc in next st, 2 sc in next st* 6 times (18 sts).

Rnd 4: *sc in next 2 sts, 2 sc in next st* 6 times (24 sts).

Rnds 5-11: sc in each st around.

Fasten off with long tail.

INNER EAR (MAKE 2)

With G6/4mm [H8/5mm; I9/5.5mm] hook and a single strand of tan yarn, ch 4.

Note: A chain 1 at the beginning of a row is for turning your work and does not count as a stitch.

Row 1: 2 sc in 2nd chain from hook, sc in next st, 2 sc in next st (5 sts).

Row 2: ch 1, turn, 2 sc in next st, sc in next 3 sts, 2 sc in next st (7 sts).

Row 3: ch 1, turn, 2 sc in next st, sc in next 5 sts, 2 sc in next st (9 sts).

Rows 4-7: ch 1, turn, sc in each st across.

Rnd 8: Do not turn. Continue working forward and sc in each st along curved edge making 3 sts in same st at corner.

Fasten off with long tail.

EYE RIM (MAKE 2)

With H8/5mm crochet hook and a single strand of tan yarn, make a magic ring, ch 1.

Rnd 1: 6 sc in ring, pull ring almost tight (6 sts).

Rnd 2: 2 sc in each st around. Place marker for beginning of rnd and move marker up as each rnd is completed (12 sts).

Rnd 3: *2 sc in next st, sc in next st* 6 times (18 sts).

Sl st in next st. Fasten off with long tail.

SNOUT

With G6/4mm [H8/5mm; I9/5.5mm] hook and a single strand of tan yarn, ch 7.

Note: A chain 1 at the beginning of a row is for turning your work and does not count as a stitch.

Row 1: 2 sc in 2nd chain from hook, sc in next 4 sts, 2 sc in next st (8 sts).

Row 2: ch 1, turn, 2 sc in next st, sc in next 6 sts, 2 sc in next st (10 sts).

Row 3: ch 1, turn, 2 sc in next st, sc in next 8 sts, 2 sc in next st (12 sts).

Row 4: ch 1, turn, 2 sc in next st, sc in next 10 sts, 2 sc in next st (14 sts).

Rows 5-9: ch 1, turn, sc in each st across.

Rnd 10: Do not turn. Continue working forward and sc in each st along curved edge making 3 sts in same st at corner.

Fasten off with long tail.

NOSE

With H8/5mm [J10/6mm: K10.5/6.5mm] hook and 2 strands of black yarn held together, make a magic ring, ch 1.

Rnd 1: 9 sc in ring, pull ring closed tight (9 sts).

Sl st in next st. Fasten off with long tail. Pull on tail to shape into a teardrop.

TOE PAD (MAKE 10)

With hook size F5/3.75mm [G6/4mm; H8/5mm] and a single strand of tan yarn, make a magic ring, ch 1.

Rnd 1: 6 sc in ring, pull ring closed tight (6 sts).

Sl st in next st. Fasten off. Pull on tail to shape work into a teardrop. Weave in ends.

HEEL PAD (MAKE 2)

With hook size F5/3.75mm [G6/4mm; H8/5mm] and a single strand of tan yarn, ch 2.

Note: A chain 1 at the beginning of a row is for turning your work and does not count as a stitch.

Row 1: 3 sc in 2nd ch from hook.

Row 2: ch 1, turn, 2 sc in next 3 sts (6 sts).

Row 3: ch 1, turn, *sc in next st, 2 sc in next st* 3 times (9 sts).

Row 4: Do not turn. Continue working forward across straight side with dc in each st across except make sl st in center st.

Sl st in next st. Fasten off. Push with fingers into a kidney bean shape. Weave in ends.

ASSEMBLY

Sew Snout to Hat. Flatten Outer Ears. Sew Inner Ears to Outer Ears. Sew Ears slightly cupped to Hat. Attach animal eyes to center of Eye Rims. Clip off excess post with wire cutters. Sew Eyes to Hat. Sew Nose to Hat and use long tail to embroider a vertical stitch from bottom of Nose to bottom of Snout. Sew Heel and Toe Pads to back side of Scarf ends with sewing needle and thread, taking shallow sts so sts don't show on front side. Weave in ends. ◆

Resources

YARN

Lion Brand
lionbrand.com
  Heartland
  Vanna's Choice

Red Heart
redheart.com
  Soft

Caron Yarn
caron.com
  Simply Soft

Michaels
michaels.com
  Lion Brand *Heartland*
  Lion Brand *Vanna's Choice*
  Red Heart *Soft*
  Caron *Simply Soft*

Joann Fabric and Craft Stores
joann.com
  Lion Brand *Heartland*
  Lion Brand *Vanna's Choice*
  Red Heart *Soft*
  Caron *Simply Soft*

NOTIONS

Joann Fabric and Craft Stores
joann.com
  Clover *Soft Touch Crochet Hook*
  Disappearing ink marking pen
  Jumbo tapestry needles
  Locking stitch markers
  Knitting counter

ANIMAL EYES

Lisa and Ed's Eye's and More
lisa.staton.home.insightbb.com

Etsy Shop 6060
etsy.com/shop/6060

CR's Crafts
crscraft.com

Amazon
amazon.com

VIDEO TUTORIALS

youtube.com
  Search on the name of the stitch or technique you want to learn.

Pinterest
pinterest.com/LindalooEnt/
  Visit my Pinterest page to view video tutorials for the stitches and techniques used in this book. Look for the boards named "Amigurumi Tutorials" and "Embroidery Tutorials".

Suggested Yarn

The following yarns are suggested for making these animal hats.

Rhinoceros

Lion Brand "Heartland"

    Color: Mount Rainier, #150

    Color: Katmai, #151

Flamingo

Lion Brand "Heartland"

    Color: Denali, #103

    Color: Biscayne, #195

    Color: Black Canyon, #153

Red Heart "Soft"

    Color: White, #4600

Turtle

Lion Brand "Heartland"

    Color: Joshua Tree, #174

    Color: Everglades, #173

Octopus

Lion Brand "Heartland"

    Color: Glacier Bay, #105

    Color: Acadia, #098

Lion

Lion Brand "Heartland"

    Color: Shenandoah, #169

    Color: Black Canyon, #153

Lion Brand "Homespun Thick & Quick"

    Color: Natural Stripes, #206

Red Heart "Soft"

    Color: White, #4600

Owl

Lion Brand "Heartland"

    Color: Big Bend, #124

    Color: Sequoia, #126

    Color: Acadia, #098

    Color: Black Canyon, #153

    Color: Bryce Canyon, #130

    Color: Shenandoah, #169

Tiger

Lion Brand "Heartland"

    Color: Yosemite, #135

    Color: Sequoia, #126

Red Heart "Soft"

    Color: White, #4600

Penguin

Lion Brand "Heartland"

    Color: Black Canyon, #153

Red Heart "Soft"

    Color: White, #4600

    Color: Tangerine, #4422

Shark

Lion Brand "Heartland"

    Color: Mount Rainier, #150

    Color: Redwood, #113

Red Heart "Soft"

    Color: White, #4600

Dog

Lion Brand "Heartland"

    Color: Mammoth Cave, #125

    Color: Grand Canyon, #122

    Color: Black Canyon, #153

Bald Eagle

Lion Brand "Heartland"

    Color: Sequoia, #126

    Color: Yellowstone, #158

    Color: Black Canyon, #153

Red Heart "Soft"

    Color: White, #4600

Ladybug

Lion Brand "Heartland"

    Color: Redwood, #113

    Color: Black Canyon, #153

Red Heart "Soft"

    Color: White, #4600

Snow Leopard

Lion Brand "Heartland"

    Color: Katmai, #151

    Color: Mount Rainier, #150

    Color: Black Canyon, #153

Rabbit

Lion Brand "Heartland"

    Color: Grand Canyon, #122

    Color: Denali, #103

Red Heart "Soft"

    Color: White, #4600

Frog

Lion Brand "Heartland"

    Color: Everglades, #173

    Color: Black Canyon, #153

    Color: Acadia, #098

Cat

Lion Brand "Heartland"

    Color: Mount Rainier, #150

    Color: Katmai, #151

    Color: Black Canyon, #153

    Color: Denali, #103

Red Heart "Soft"

    Color: White, #4600

Mallard

Lion Brand "Heartland"

    Color: King's Canyon, #180

    Color: Sequoia, #126

    Color: Yellowstone, #158

    Color: Black Canyon, #153

Red Heart "Soft"

    Color: White, #4600

    Color: Tangerine, #4422

Sheep

Lion Brand "Heartland"

    Color: Acadia, #098

    Color: Denali, #103

    Color: Black Canyon, #153

Bee

Lion Brand "Heartland"

    Color: Yellowstone, #158

    Color: Black Canyon, #153

    Color: Acadia, #098

Bear

Lion Brand "Heartland"

    Color: Sequoia, #126

    Color: Grand Canyon, #122

    Color: Black Canyon, #153

Other books by Linda Wright

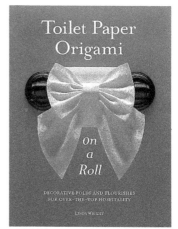

LINDA WRIGHT studied textiles and clothing design at the Pennsylvania State University. She is the author of various handicraft books including the bestselling *Toilet Paper Origami* and its companion book, *Toilet Paper Origami On a Roll*; the innovative *Toilet Paper Crafts*; and numerous works of whimsical amigurumi-style crochet. To learn more about these fun-filled books, visit:

tporigami.com   **pinterest.com/LindalooEnt**   **amazon.com**

Notes

CPSIA information can be obtained
at www.ICGtesting.com
Printed in the USA
BVHW021146031221
622917BV00007B/43